A Shelter in the Garden

A Shelter in the Garden

Playhouses, Treehouses, Gazebos, Sheds, and Other Outdoor Structures

Pierre Nessmann
Photographs by Brigitte and Philippe Perdereau

Stewart, Tabori & Chang
New York

Published in 2009 by Stewart, Tabori & Chang
An imprint of Harry N. Abrams, Inc.

Library of Congress Cataloging-in-Publication Data

Nessmann, Pierre.
  A Shelter in the Garden : playhouses, treehouses, gazebos, sheds, and other outdoor structures / by Pierre Nessmann ; [photographs by] Brigitte and Philippe Perdereau ; translated by Krister Swartz.
     p. cm.
  Includes index.
  ISBN 978-1-58479-771-5
  1. Garden structures—Design and construction. I. Perdereau, Brigitte. II. Perdereau, Philippe. III. Swartz, Krister. IV. Title.
  TH4961.N47 2009
   728'.9—dc22
                         2008043074

Design by Éléonor Gerbier

Translated by Krister Swartz

English-language edition:
Magali Veillon, Project Manager
Miranda Ottewell, Editor
Shawn Dahl, Designer
Jules Thomson, Production Manager

The text of this book was composed in Profile and Today.

Printed and bound in China
10 9 8 7 6 5 4 3 2 1

HNA
harry n. abrams, inc.
a subsidiary of La Martinière Groupe
115 West 18th Street
New York, NY 10011
www.hnabooks.com

Contents

Introduction

For many of us, building a garden shelter is just a fond childhood memory, or a fun thing to do for our children now that we have grown up. But why not take the plunge, and create this retreat of youthful dreams for ourselves now? In these pages you will find examples of structures to suit all styles of gardens, tips on how to make them, and perhaps a few ideas that you have never even thought of—leafy sanctuaries, cabins set on wheels, canvas tents. Whether you want a place to store garden tools, a hut to play in, or a simple decorative structure, you'll find it in this book. So let's do it—let's build a little something for ourselves!

A Childhood Treehouse

In the spring of 1975, the ramshackle shelter I put together in the tangled boughs of a weeping willow, planted ten years earlier by my father on the occasion of my birth, finally took the shape of a real treehouse. I couldn't say that this was my first attempt to build it, since for years I had busied myself each summer, more than ten feet off the ground, tweaking my makeshift collection of milled planks and chestnut branches gleaned from the nearby woods. To my great frustration, it remained a primitive structure, no more than a simple platform that I reached with a ladder—and that, ramshackle as it was, I more than once knocked to the ground!

But it was there that, on a beautiful day in April, my dream of an actual treehouse became a reality. Finally I was in possession of the real thing, complete with a frame that delicately rested against the strong branches of my tree, sporting a planked floor, walls, and even topped with a steep roof that gave this much-anticipated shelter the silhouette of a tepee. It was the height of luxury; one of the walls even had a window, with small glass panes salvaged from a demolition site, and a view over the Vosges! Once it was built, I set about insulating my refuge with pieces of cardboard painted white, hung typical red-and-white Alsatian curtains in the windows, and set up some camping equipment inside. Perched up there in my tree, I lived in a world of joyous adventure.

Unfortunately, my wonderful weeping willow, a tree I once thought so robust, did not survive. Its soft wood could not resist the assaults of wood-boring insects, of scabs, and above all, of the passing of time. For me as well, time flowed by, and today, designing gardens populated by new trees has become my vocation. So that, one day, I can realize my new secret dream: to build, in one of them, a little something for Antoine, Simon, and Victor.

Two Chairs and a Blanket

From our earliest childhood we are possessed by the desire to erect little structures to play in, and long after we have turned our minds to adult concerns, the idea still appeals to us. What is this innate attachment to these simple, some might say primitive, dwellings? Is it the desire to take refuge in a cozy human-size nest? A need to escape from the harsh realities of this world? There are probably a thousand different explanations. Some people have fulfilled this ancient dream on their own, while others have stumbled upon it by lucky chance—and a growing number have even made creating such structures their livelihood. For the majority of us, though, this dream is still only an abstraction, far away and seemingly unachievable. And yet, to cherish this basic human desire is the first step toward one day seeing it become a reality: you don't need to have woods or a large garden to build a little shelter of your own. Whether on the roof of a large apartment building, nestled in the hollow of a small city garden, or—why not?—set into the center of a building, atriumlike, as part of renovating a room, that place of our childhood dreams can flourish far beyond the limits of the garden.

The Garden Shelter in All Its Forms

ORIGINS

There is not a forest, vineyard, or agricultural region that is not dotted with some form of small build-ing. Makeshift shelters such as the woodcutter's huts in central France or the stout drystone structures of Provence have always offered farmers, woodsmen, and shepherds shelter during storms, protection from the sun in the hottest part of the day, or simply a place to eat lunch near the workplace. Moving from these rural districts, where they were primarily ephemeral and sometimes perfunctory structures, these shelters have become common in ornamental gardens. Landscape artists and architects who wanted to better integrate such structures into their new settings have given them a more sophisti-cated appearance, adapting them to the style and architecture of their surroundings. Trellised arbors, sanctuaries of carved wood, and gemlike little masonry follies were scattered throughout the gardens of the Italian Renaissance, then adapted to the geometric gardens of the French, before they ornamented the Romantic parkland landscapes of England. Placed at strategic points in the design, such buildings can create a focal point, balance a landscape composition, or draw the eye to a distant view. But these structures are not only the prerogative of the grand public parks or the expansive gardens of the gentry; old work sheds, chicken coops, and other small structures have always played a role in the gardens of our grandparents. Today, after several decades of neglect, these ephemeral buildings are now all the rage, attracting a large following. Is this but a passing fancy, or a lasting interest? No one can say. One thing, however, is sure: the new popularity of these fragile structures has encouraged their preservation and restoration. And the safeguarding of these everyday bits of our heritage, whose walls enclose the story of the life of our countryside and our gardens, contributes to our own larger history.

SIZE AND STYLE

A small toolshed or chest might fit nicely into the small garden or on a patio, but it is not the best option for sheltering plants or transplanting. A larger garden shed offers not only a place to keep fertilizers, potting soil, tools, and plants, but also a pleasant place to potter around and pass the time. Indeed, some gardeners end up converting their sheds into veritable living spaces. Decorated and fitted out with some comfortable furniture, these utilitarian storage areas can become focal points for relaxing or entertaining. And why stop there? It's inevitable, in the spirit of our times: many of these constructions, growing larger and larger, are today beginning to look like small houses. So what about regulations?

AS FOR THE LAW . . .

Each state has its own laws on sheds, covering zoning ordinances, building codes, deed restrictions, building permits, siding materials, and so on. It is prudent to closely check local building codes and ordinances before starting to plan or install any garden structures. Some sheds, like other structures, require the proper permits, without which they can be considered illegal. The rules may dictate the total space that a structure can take up, time restrictions for construction, and materials. Some housing associations also have their own rules and regulations that must be followed. A little investigation beforehand will prevent much grief later.

Garden
Structures

Perched in trees or solidly anchored to the ground, made of straw, wood, or canvas, set out in the open or hidden in a quiet corner, used for storage, for show, or only for play, garden structures have a multitude of functions, and come in as many styles and models as there are owners, users, or residents of the garden. And when we speak of residents, we include those that can be somewhat unexpected: domestic animals, birds, and insects also have the right to take refuge in our gardens. As a reflection of its owner or creator, each structure is unique. We should start with a little general survey.

Toolsheds
and Outhouses

The smallest structure in which to store things in the garden is the vertical version of the tool chest—in other words, the toolshed. Because of its small size, however, it only offers room for tools, and thus provides no shelter for the gardener. Another garden structure is reserved for a very specific, though undeniably practical, use, this time for people, not tools: the outhouse. These small buildings, once common in both country and city, have been disappearing since the nineteenth century from both our gardens and our courtyards. Those remaining exist only because gardeners have taken it on themselves to preserve them and cleverly reconvert them to garden sheds.

Covered in greenery, this shed has the appearance and proportions of an old-time outhouse and solves the storage problem in a small space. Sided in painted wooden planks and topped with a tin roof, it provides shelter in bad weather for fertilizers, potting soil, tools, and garden accessories, while at the same time adding an original and decorative note to the garden; set into its door is a mirror that reflects the surrounding flowers and greenery.

Above: Adorned with a decorative frieze, this shed in the style of a little chalet actually holds a composting toilet that produces part of the fertilizer used in the garden. **Facing page, left:** The discreet broom closet, so practical inside our houses, is perfect out here for sheltering tools and garden materials behind a soft screen of greenery. **Facing page, right:** To add a bit of elegance to a toolshed, it's enough to give it the look of a porte-cochère, with an arched roof that evokes the entrance to a subterranean cave or one of those icehouses of old.

At the Back of the Garden

Descendants of latrines, tiny shelters no bigger than a closet can be the perfect thing for cramped gardens, or any area where room for storing garden equipment is scarce. Whether discreetly set against a wall or right out in plain view in the heart of the garden, these little sheds always have the same layout: four walls of identical dimension with a door in one side, topped with a sloped shed roof. With a footprint of about ten square feet, this standard model, widely available in do-it-yourself kits, allows only limited customization. For a more personalized structure that you can adapt more easily to the style of your particular garden, you might consider a custom-built structure, if this is allowed in your area. Double doors, arched roofs, and deeper eaves under which you can store wood are some useful and decorative additions; you can also choose your own color scheme for the siding, whether to make your building stand out or blend in with its surroundings.

A WORD OF ADVICE

The outhouse might belong to a past time, but composting toilets are becoming more and more popular. One simple technique relies on a sprinkling of sawdust or wood shavings after each use to neutralize odors and begin the composting process. The mixture can then be regularly collected and dumped on a compost pile for use in the garden. This is a great water saver, especially in the city, where 35 percent of the potable water ends up being flushed into the sewer.

Garden Sheds

An accessory indispensable to any gardener worth his salt, the garden shed is the reflection of its owner. Whether our grandfathers' secret lair crammed with a thousand things—not all of them useful!—or our grandmothers' quiet getaway in the form of a little cottage, these buildings are first and foremost designed to hold all of one's garden equipment out of the weather and close to where it will be needed the most: out by the kitchen garden. In fact, along with the compost heap, the cold frame, the greenhouse, and the well, the garden shed is one of the most common sights next to the garden patch. However, this very practical shed has many other uses, such as storing garden furniture or overwintering tender perennials; these days many people go even further, using it as a place for children to play, or their parents to relax.

The increasing appeal of the garden shed these days has earned it a place right out in plain view. The traditional toolshed has been revisited as an exercise in style—here, a shed in the form of a cube is modern in its architecture, yet conservative in its use of pine plank siding; left untreated, the pine boards have weathered to the ashy gray of an old lean-to.

Grandmother's Garden Shed

Adorned with small-paned windows and painted shutters, and covered in garlands of flowers, this is the feminine, poetic version of the shed. The interior is still a functional storage space, but its exterior mirrors the style of its user—elegant, like our grandmothers. Without delving too much into clichés, it is enough to note that buildings maintained by gardeners have a few notable characteristics. Whether we are talking about prefabricated models or custom-built ones, all are embellished with small personal touches that elevate them to the status of decorative elements. Architectural details (frames, railings, friezes) are set off by vivid colors and climbing plants, and the most prosaic elements (foundations and gutters) are cleverly disguised under festoons of flowers and draping foliage. The penchant for embellishment is, of course, not limited to the building, but extends out into the area around it as well. Garden equipment, rainwater collectors, and composters are hidden behind verdant screens and flowering bushes, making the total effect even more seductive. Such a building often becomes a meeting place for all those who use the garden.

Facing page: Over time, "grandmother's" garden shed becomes adorned with decorative elements that more than justify its position at the center of the garden. Becoming a major decorative element in its own right, it replaces the regular geometry of garden beds with more romantic clothing: flowers and roses. **Above:** Partially hidden behind a rich growth of shrubs and climbing roses, this shed's board siding has faded, giving it the fine look of old paneling.

Grandfather's Garden Shed

In contrast to the feminine version, this type of shed is recognizable by its purely functional look. No question of burdening oneself with ornamentation here; leave aesthetics out of it. These sheds are designed above all else to store and protect garden tools and supplies. More often than not, they are also used as a sort of laboratory, where ingenious prototypes are developed to increase yield or to enhance the performance of a particular garden tool. These activities result in such an accumulation of bits and pieces, one can't help but wonder if the purpose of this disorderly spread of so many different objects is simply to ward off approaching intruders! Everything is useful, or will be one day. . . . With generous, unhampered openings to give access to cumbersome materials, these buildings, more often than not, have no surrounding plantings, the easier to maintain the siding and roofing. Without vegetation to ornament them, they are best left to a remote corner of the garden and camouflaged by bushes, not only to soften their presence in the rest of the garden, but also to preserve the mysterious atmosphere that is part of their appeal.

Above: The masculine version of the garden shed often doubles as a trial laboratory for the garden. This function transforms the area around the building into a storage zone, so that it is best kept hidden from the principal views in the garden.

Above: Functionality, practicality, and ease of maintenance embody the attitude behind these buildings, whose facades are free of any vegetation. Earth and garden beds are discouraged and often undesirable around such a bare building, which as a result often looks as if it was built just yesterday.

The Stylish Shed

The time of the prefab tin shed or the standardized little imitation Alpine chalet is long past—and that's all the better for our gardens, in which, over the past few years, these little structures have been elevated from the merely functional to decorative elements. From modest sheds made of wood patinated by time, to gleaming structures adorned in bright and extravagant colors, they have brought high style to the garden. Without losing their basic purpose as storage units, they often stand squarely in the center of the garden as a focus of interest. With architecture similar to that of a small house and spacious interiors, sheds are fitted out for comfort (with insulation, heating, and furniture) and pleasure (with a sauna or Jacuzzi) as perfect little living spaces. And just as the interiors are well cared for and contemporary in style, the exteriors of these hideaways are finished with choice materials, color washes, elegant patinas, and of course various architectural elements. Here there is no question of using doors or windows on a smaller scale and of mediocre quality, as with traditional garden sheds; instead, these structures make use of the full range of materials available for house construction. With their accurate proportions and quality materials, these buildings gain the look and style of a true house, around which it is only natural to install a garden of character. Perennials, flowering shrubs, and grasses work together to elaborate a refined décor, alongside original and innovative landscape materials.

Above: With a coat of bright paint, an ordinary run-down shed finds a second youth with a bold design style. **Facing page, top:** With its French doors of the same quality as those used in a house, this building goes beyond the status of garden shed to that of a refined little cottage, its stylishness underlined by filmy fabric screens. **Facing page, bottom:** With a hipped wood shingle roof, this building takes on the shape of a traditional residence, but preserves the spirit of the shed by its dimensions and the use of wood siding painted with a light color wash.

The "Green" Shed

These sheds lend themselves to all types of styles and allow for some architectural extravagances that give us a taste of the garden shed designs of the future. Inspired by contemporary architecture, these simple and refined geometric buildings use wood for their structure and facing, thus placing them halfway between traditional sheds and the wood-frame houses popular today. If these buildings share a superficial similarity to traditional sheds, both being built of wood, and with a name in common, the similarities end there, as these buildings expand on the innovative concepts taken from climate-conscious and environmentally friendly housing. Designed with large glass panels that give them a resolutely modern look, and that also provide passive solar heat, much as in a greenhouse, this new class of shed is often topped with a living roof and equipped with rainwater collectors. Created with eco-certified materials, they use the same techniques—double-hung windows, ample insulation, and ventilation systems—that are used in larger buildings, so they benefit from the technological advances that put them at the forefront of progress, but take them farther and farther away from the traditional garden shed.

A WORD OF ADVICE

Be careful that your enthusiasm for green construction does not lead you too far away from creating a garden shed, and closer to building what local inspectors may consider a house. Even if the building is constructed entirely of wood and by definition can be easilly dismantled, its dimensions, its style, and its impact on the countryside may necessitate a work order or construction permit. In lieu of engaging the services of an architect or scaling back the ambition of your project, remember that a garden shed, as long as you keep it to a modest size, can be a perfect application of the principles of green construction and sustainable development.

Facing page: Built of red cedar whose ruddy hue has faded over time to reveal gray nuances, this contemporary flat-roofed shed has large glass panels that open onto the garden, making it closer in spirit to a traditional conservatory than a garden shed. **Above:** The contemporary geometric look of the long wall of this building, its wood siding grayed over time, stands in sharp contrast to a setting of natural greenery. Part greenhouse, part shed, it is fitted with large doors that afford easy access. A glass orangery at one end can be used to overwinter tender perennials.

The Playhouse

Miniature garden cottages and huts, besides being used for storage and to nurture plants, can act as perfect hideaways for the very young. A playhouse may first be used only for hide-and-seek, but soon the space becomes a great place for picnics and other improvised parties. This, in turn, leads to its use as a little residence, with more sophisticated and comfortable interior decoration. Little by little, chairs with plenty of cushions, a coffee table, and curtains are introduced, a transformation that forces the gardener to share the space with small new occupants. When the last tools are shoved aside by furniture, it's time to begin construction on a new garden shed! Children's playhouses come in numerous styles, and all have the advantage of being scaled to a modest size. Not only doors and windows, but even furniture, can be adapted to the very small, and guarantee use without trouble or mishap. On the other hand, after a few years, the space will become tight; the children, too cramped, will end up deserting the place. Thus, it may be a better idea to opt for a traditional garden shed. If it seems a little oversize for its first few years of use as a children's house, it can, on the other hand, be used for a longer time, when the children grow out of it and it is converted back into a proper toolshed.

Above: Built in an enclosed garden, this little playhouse with simple openings is surrounded by luxurious vegetation. Made of particleboard painted azure blue, it looks like something right out of *Alice in Wonderland*.

The "XXL" Shed

Not quite full-size buildings and yet a bit too large to be called sheds, which they otherwise resemble: little outbuildings in the country—once henhouses or small barns—as well as disused garages and sheds make up this popular group. They are often already classified as annexes; saving their owners from needing to obtain a construction permit before they begin building. Furthermore, no other step is needed when it is time to renovate them, as long as their designation hasn't changed. Finally, in addition to their appeal as artifacts harking back to a rural lifestyle, these buildings offer ample space to shelter and store materials, tinker in, or play in. Rescuing them from the ravages of time by restoring them is thus well worth the effort. However, the size of these buildings makes work on them much more involved than with a regular garden shed. As with residential buildings, it is important to work under cover—that is, to make sure that the structure is protected from bad weather so that exposed roofing or siding is not damaged. As these sheds are often built of wood, it is also necessary to make sure that runoff water does not gather in stagnant pools near the foundation or lower part of the wood siding. Treat the wooden frame and siding to protect it against wood-boring insects, and give yourself time to restore the building properly before using it again.

Above: Transformed into an orangery, this summer shed has many openings to allow in ample light. The windows open outward so that they can be used easily without disturbing the plants inside.

Raised Garden Structures

Life in the clouds! It is an old dream that we share, a fantasy deeply embedded in us all. Whether it's the wish to fly, the desire to rise up into the heights, or the simple curiosity to see life from above, taking to the heavens has always fascinated and attracted us. And so, small or large, with the help of a few trees, we build structures that give us the illusion we can do this. From terraces raised on stilts to tree forts built in the crux of branches, there are all kinds of ways to "live in the clouds." But we must be prudent and safe. The higher up we build, the more complex it becomes, and the more we need to enlist the help of professionals.

This roomy expanse of wood decking raised above a hillside, accessed by a footbridge that meanders around the tree trunks, offers an exceptional panorama from a breathtaking vantage. The absence of guardrails on the bridge and deck enhances the impression of freedom and expanse, but makes the deck off-limits to young children.

Building on Posts

Lifting a building only a few feet off the ground is sometimes enough to give the impression of a perched or raised structure. This technique is highly recommended when a structure will be used by children, to lessen the risk of a bad fall. Simply setting an ordinary existing shed, for example, on top of a mound of dirt can give it the feeling of a perched structure. The sides of the mound can be hidden with vegetation, and stairs added to lead up to the entrance. If shaping a mound of dirt doesn't work for you, the structure could also be set on concrete footers, cinder blocks, or wooden posts. Raising your structure off the ground also creates a crawlspace for ventilation and lessens the risk of damage caused by moisture. For reasons of stability, rather than stacking up two or even three layers of blocks, it may be best to attach the structure to round or squared posts solidly anchored into the ground. At this height, it is also a good idea to build a deck on one side, or even a wraparound porch or deck, which will not only make the place look nicer but add to the usable space and comfort.

Facing page: Perched two feet or so off the ground and attached to posts, this wooden playhouse for kids, with a corrugated tin roof and a front deck, is high enough off the ground to rub shoulders with low-lying branches of small trees and to create the illusion of a place up in the treetops. **Above:** Two steps are enough to give the impression of height and the illusion that this shed looks down onto the garden. A surrounding deck amplifies this sensation and heightens the contrast of the drop-off.

It's not just children who can appreciate a slightly raised structure, and the use of pole construction is not exclusively for traditional buildings, as this shed shows, placed as it is in the heart of a contemporary garden. Here, the starkly cube-shaped structure is inserted into a nook carved right into the enclosing hedge, integrating it into the garden. Almost two feet off the ground, the assembly of shed and deck, which has something of the uncompromising outline of a construction-site cabin, makes an interesting object to look at in its own right, while offering a counterpoint to the nearby landscaping. In its color, its proportion, and the sharp horizontal lines of its wood siding, the shed relates effectively to the surrounding hardscaping, the brick used for the low retaining wall, and the lines of the wooden walkway. Far from anything Robin Hood and his band of merry men might have used, it demonstrates that an elevated shed is not only for traditional gardens, but works equally to enhance the spirit of contemporary design.

Facing page and above: The placement of a shed in a small space like this—set within a hedge marking a property line, and cleverly occupying the space left by the removal of a dying conifer—may mean it requires a building permit. However, as it is only slightly higher than the existing fence, and blends nicely into it, there should be no objection from the neighbors.

Building on Straw Bales

Straw-bale construction is at once an ancient method of wall-building and a new technique that is the current darling of "green" builders. The straw bales that are abundant at harvest time in those areas where wheat is grown make an excellent material for building or supporting a shed. A straw bale will not rot when it is kept dry, but will eventually decompose when it is left uncovered and exposed to bad weather. Since a shed built of straw can withstand the rain for only a few months, these structures are temporary ones. But straw-bale construction still gives you the chance, during summer vacation, to build something completely new and original. Oat straw is more impermeable to water than wheat straw, which disintegrates quickly, but in both cases look for small square bales, which will be easier to transport and to work with than large or round bales. After you've acquired and transported your precious bundles, you need only to stack them to make the walls of your shed, or use them for a platform to build on. Though it might take a bit of hard work to raise the shed walls, it does not take much thought or know-how. To make sure that your structure is sound, be sure to stagger your bales and to reinforce them with a few stakes, or rebar, driven into the ground.

Above and facing page: Large round bales can be used to build platforms on which to place porches, footbridges, and wood shelters. While they are stable and will last a few years, they can be cumbersome and difficult to transport and maneuver into place.

Building on Stilts

Inspired by the rice huts of the Asian continent, the granaries of the mountainous regions of France, or the raised huts called *mazots* in the Swiss Alps, sheds on stilts have wooden frames that are raised several feet to protect them from flooding and from the wildlife that may be attracted to what is inside. Supported on posts rather than attached to tree branches, these traditional structures make great models for building a shed somewhat like a tree fort. But though they don't need to be built around a tree, these sheds, often very attractive, are still somewhat complex to build. The weight of the structure and distribution of the weight on a few poles makes building this a little more complicated than a simple shed built on the ground. Unlike a tree house, where branches offer a stable and fixed support, the frame of a shed on stilts must handle a shifting load, and must therefore be equipped with braces and buttresses carefully placed to prevent the structure from collapsing like a house of cards. The construction of this type of structure should be entrusted to a knowledgeable professional in order to lessen the risk of accident.

Above: This shed made of woven chestnut cane coated with cob (a mixture of clay and straw) and roofed with wooden shingles offers a quiet nest in the middle of the forest. **Right, and facing page:** Despite the luxurious use of bamboo, palms, and grasses, this typical Laotian habitat is not in Asia, but in the heart of the French countryside!

Building over Water

The shanties, grass huts, and other cabins characteristic of faraway countries may be used as a source of inspiration because of their unusual and exotic look. But really it is the use of water, more than the originality of their architecture, that gives these buildings their unique feel. While they are built on a river or in a marsh or floodplain in their country of origin, in our gardens, most of these structures are built right over or at the edge of an ornamental pond, which creates the illusion that the building is floating on water with tropical plantings around it. The connection to the original dwellings is heightened by the use of vegetation—river plants and aquatic grasses—that create the atmosphere of a riverbank. A final touch is the use of a footbridge to reach the entrance, or a pontoon crossing the water, which cultivates the impression of a faraway refuge. The exotic atmosphere is also enhanced by the use of natural materials and vegetation like palms and thatch for the roof and reeds for the walls.

Facing page and above: More than the materials and design of an outdoor structure, plants contribute to the success of tropical decor. Here, papyrus and aquatic grasses in the water, and tree ferns, bananas, and palms on the banks come together to create an exotic scene. These somewhat tropical plants prefer mild climates, however, and would have to be replaced with hardy perennials in a colder one.

The Treehouse

Part of the reason many of us are drawn to a place up in the treetops is the urge to become part of that universe of leaves, to enter into that intimacy of branches, with the birds as our neighbors. But to take to the heights is also to look out over the world without being seen. Every child dreams of climbing up into the trees, with a hodgepodge collection of sticks, to build a tree house perched up in the sky. Even as we grow older, the desire to play Swiss Family Robinson is still always lurking there just under the surface, revealing itself even in our attraction to shelters up in trees. Why deprive ourselves? For the resourceful and handy, building a treehouse is child's play, as long, of course, as you keep safety in mind. If you are less skillful, find someone to help. Whether you do it yourself or hire someone do to it, you will still need the necessary support structure—that is, a tree, or a couple of them, in which to build. Back when you were a kid, you may have cared little about these trees, about their health and how your building would affect their growth. But today we have done away with those large and rustic anchors that damaged wood and weakened a tree's crown; through respect for the tree, we have developed new techniques. Because the tree is a living thing, we must think carefully before going up into its branches. The distribution of weight, the support, and the fixtures of your structure should not be left to chance. Everything should be done to respect the tree and to allow its trunk, as well as its branches, to grow normally, without hindrance.

A WORD OF ADVICE

Safety is a given that should not be neglected when designing a tree house. Falls, even at low heights, can have serious consequences, and are one of the most common causes of domestic injury. Because tree houses are so popular, and because of the dangers that come with them, in the future these types of structures may be regulated. Just like swimming pools, whose access is formally regulated today, tree-house-type structures beyond a certain height could also be subject to regulation. In any case, if the garden is used by young children, it is best to control access to the structure by using, for example, a ladder that can be removed.

Facing page, top: A treehouse with a deck offers room for more people. It also reinforces the load-bearing structure by driving additional support poles into the ground. **Facing page, bottom:** When trunks are close enough, it is better to distribute the load among several of the most vigorous and healthy trees.

Above and facing page: Attached to the ancient trunk of a lime tree, the floor of this structure, covered with a simple reed roof and secured with a rope balustrade, is supported by thick posts to distribute the weight and take some of it off the tree. Here, the habit of the tree, with its vertical branches, did not allow for a structure inside its crown. Wrapping the structure around the tree, then, was the best option, preserving the life of the tree, and offering more, and more comfortable, space for people.

The Suspended Deck

Essentially this is just a raised garden shed left unfinished, without walls or roof. Suspended decks can still function much like the decks built off houses—that is, for relaxation, mealtimes, a gathering place, and so on—only here they are perched a few feet, or more, off the ground, and often far from the house. A raised deck must be equipped with handrails and stairs, or a ramp with a gate to control access, especially if the garden is used by small children. They work best tucked into the heart of a grove of trees or under the canopy of one, to give the deck natural protection from the sun's rays and from insects. The decking boards, fastened to a frame suspended on posts driven into the ground, can be laid so that the trunks of trees rise through the deck; the resulting effect of being suspended in the treetops will add greatly to the magic of the structure.

Facing page and above: About four feet off the ground, this deck has a surface of several dozen square feet and fills the space between the trees, while allowing their trunks to pierce through the decking. This aspect of the design should be well thought out, since the trunks may eventually expand and damage the deck as the trees grow. A little space should be left between the bark and the boards, which should be well sanded, and the supporting structure should be laid out to give enough space around the trunks to let them grow larger without displacing the decking.

In a Green Shade

Temporary structures made of woven branches and stems have always existed. Even as long ago as the Middle Ages, makeshift shelters provided protection from the blazing sun during the day. To begin with, they had a very limited life span, as they were made with freshly cut branches that dried extremely quickly, making them somewhat precarious. It was not long, however, before these vegetative structures, made from branches and leaves, were transformed. Light frames yielded to more solid construction, and the curtain of leaves was replaced with climbing plants that were a little more permanent. Today, the foliage of climbers hides a light frame of wood or steel, and the bower's very decorative appearance fits in well with the natural spirit of modern-day gardens.

Because of their suppleness, chestnut canes work well for all kinds of projects, like here, where they define an ogive that delicately crowns a framework made of larger poles of the same wood. The twining branches of crimson glory vine (*Vitis coignetiae*), star jasmine (*Trachelospermum jasminioides*), and chocolate vine (*Akebia quinata*) discreetly rise into the framer, which will be hidden under a thick blanket of leaves after a few years, forming a refuge from prying eyes and the sun.

The Living Shelter

Willow (or osier) canes, commonly shaped and dried to make garden furniture, are these days also used "in the green," or living. Willow canes can be planted in the earth, where they will take root, establish themselves, and leaf out. The legendary suppleness of their wood lends itself well to manipulation, so it can soon be formed into a simple and permanent leafy structure, creating a living artwork. The flexibility of willow allows it to be woven, twisted, knotted, or crisscrossed into numerous designs, but domes, like igloos, and tunnels are the easiest to make. Simply cut branches no more than one year old in the fall and plant them in a bit of earth from December to May. The roots will sprout rapidly; new branches come not long after, and in the following spring will begin to leaf out to the point that one or two trimmings will be necessary to shape them. The resulting little structures are self-sufficient, and need not be maintained like the framework of a house. On the other hand, larger designs, usually made with hornbeam or beech, need to be attached to a support.

Facing page: Two species of willow have curly branches: *Salix erythroflexuosa* and *S. matsudana "Tortuosa."* Both root well and are suitable for arranging into structures with dense weaves, but their vigorous growth makes it necessary to prune them often with shears, from June to October, to keep them neat. **Above:** *Salix vinimalis* can be bent into all kinds of forms but needs a support to make acute angles. Here, the branches are trained into shape, then attached to metal to keep the form perfect.

Above: Hornbeam (*Carpinus betulus*), like beech (*Fagus sylvatica*), lends itself to training and is sturdy enough to make sizable living structures. To get a neat and tidy appearance, however, you will need to start by fabricating a permanent structure, here in steel, to support the
young branches, then maintain the shape with regular pruning.

Top: From the inside, it is still possible to see the iron framework that these trees have been trained over; after a few years, their branches and trunks will have grown thick enough not to need additional support. **Above:** The long, thin, deep brown branches of willow (*Salix triandra*) bend easily and can be shaped into a leafy tunnel. Without support, however, the weight of the leaves can cause the whole structure to sag.

The Arbor

The arbor is a modest structure, often fanciful, made with light materials that climbing plants can clamber over, creating a shaded area in the garden or forming an extension to a room of the house. Steel or wood pillars support an open horizontal framework of canes, bamboo, or metal rods, covered, sometimes, with a simple network of wire. This grid supports the twining branches of climbing plants that, after a few years, will entirely cover the arbor, hiding the frame itself with their foliage. The impression produced is much like that of a bower, since garlands of vegetation cover the sides. This leafy covering creates a dappled shade from spring to autumn, when the leaves fall, revealing the shape of the frame through the winter. Arbors are at their best during the growing season, when shade is most desirable in the garden, and at other times provide only discreet sculptural forms.

A WORD OF ADVICE

When building an arbor, pay attention to the surface you wish to cover, and more precisely the area that should be shaded. Remember to ensure that you have shade when and where you want it , the sun does not follow the same path in every season, Also, make sure the structure is at least seven and a half feet high, so that it will be easy to stand and walk under it without getting tangled up in branches or leaves. Finally, take care to train climbers carefully up over the structure, and keep an eye on the weight of the plants, not only as they grow, but also after a rain. You can lighten the load by trimming vines annually and by removing old or errant branches.

Facing page: This arbor, made of a mesh of bamboo canes, is too light to support heavy climbers, like kiwi (*Actinidia*). Over time, the weight of the creeper may bend the structure. **Top:** A few bamboo canes, bound together, create a haphazard support for a wisteria with its hanging seedpods. **Above:** A more complicated structure, this arbor forms an A-frame roof similar to that on a house, which will soon be buried under the exuberant foliage of morning glory.

The Pergola

Originally from Italy, the classical pergola is a small structure made of horizontal beams resting on wooden or stone pillars and designed to support climbing plants. By extension, all garden structures open to the sky and covered with vegetation on a horizontal roof frame tend to be called pergolas, a looser definition that can lead to confusion. Delicate or imposing, pergolas can be attached to one side of a house to create verdant shelters, or they can make a freestanding summer room in a corner of the garden. Elongated pergolas can create a shady walkway. Larger than arbors, they are also more sturdy. Their horizontal beams, designed principally to give shade from the sun, perhaps even more than the vegetation, are substantial enough to provide some shelter from the rain. As a result, they can easily take on the function of supplementary rooms, while retaining the garden shelter feel with rustic materials, simple furniture, and the presence of climbing plants.

Facing page: Over a walkway of slate shards, a simple pergola of vertical and horizontal poles supports a roof of woven chestnut canes. The dappled shade is perfect for plants that may scorch in too much sun, such as abutilons, in a Mediterranean region. **Above:** A wonderful extra living room open to the garden, this pergola has a horizontal structure covered with a roof, creating a space protected from both glaring sun and bad weather that can be used all year long.

Top: Emerging from a carpet of feather grass (*Stipa sp.*) and verbascum at the heart of a xeriscapic garden, four pillars support a light structure that covers a dining area in dappled shade. **Above:** In the south of France, a screen made of the stalks of giant reed (*Arundo donax*) bound with wire is used as a windbreak as well as for shade. Bamboo canes could be used to similar effect.

Top: Without making the space too dark, a reed screen filters the sun's rays and casts dappled shade under a pergola. Brushwood fence panels or woven willow could also be used for this type of structure, but these weather rapidly when exposed to bright sun and must be replaced every two or three years. **Above:** Entirely covered by a tiled roof, this structure is not a pergola but a portico or loggia. Though the space underneath may be a little dark, the roof allows the area to be used all year long.

Rest Shelters

Just big enough to provide shelter for a chair or bench, a rest shelter provides a place for the weary gardener to take a little break, or for the stroller to pause and contemplate the landscape. Whether a simple screen of branches and leaves, like a green cradle, or a wood-framed structure like a little pergola, such a sanctuary offers room for only one or two to sit. However simple or small, these invaluable nooks can fit in just about anywhere—on a high spot overlooking the garden, for example, or at the end of a garden walk, so the borders along it can be appreciated at leisure. Some rest shelters, more modest and discreet, might be tucked away at the heart of a garden; their value is not in the view they command but in the quiet, intimate retreat they provide.

A rattan chair weathered by time, a few branches tied together in the form of a tepee, the fragrant flowers of honeysuckle, and Japanese wind chimes come together to create an enchanting little shelter. An ideal spot to take refuge in the heart of the garden, this green nest in the shrubbery offers a chance to get away from it all for a few moments, reveling in the intimacy of nature.

The Topiary Nook

After you have set up a bench in the perfect place, perhaps overlooking a vista of perennial borders, it can begin to seem a little exposed out there in the middle of the garden. So you start thinking about shrubs or climbers to plant around it, to give it an anchor and a feeling of protection. A few years later, your plantings have thrived, and the original bench has become almost hidden under a jungle of foliage and flowers, changing the atmosphere in unexpected ways. Perhaps it's a little out of hand; now you will need to get out the shears or clippers and pare down this tangle of greenery. When you've finished this job, the natural vault of twigs and leaves thus created may be strikingly similar to the leafy bowers of Renaissance gardens. This is how, without their makers even realizing it, the first topiary shelters often appear in the garden. To keep this feeling of a soft nest, remove old or dead wood and trim lightly every year.

Above: Climbers, like this honeysuckle, are a good way to softly frame a bench with a little greenery, but they will need some kind of structure to support them. Another option would be to plant shrubs and train a few of the most vigorous branches to create an arched frame of foliage and flowers.

Wickerwork and Willow Cane

Traditionally used dry for basket making and green to make fascines (bundles of willow rods used to make a hedge or reinforce a riverbank), willow canes have been used in the garden for some years now in a number of ways. They can be pressure-treated in an autoclave, as is often done with pine, giving them exceptional resistance to weathering and decay. This treatment considerably lengthens their life span, which would ordinarily be only a few years outside. After the branches have been stripped of their bark, they are woven and pressure-treated, which gives them their beige tint. The simplest pieces to create, and the most common, are uniform flat panels, but arched structures are the most beautiful and spectacular—and the most expensive. Working with willow "in the green" is another intriguing technique. Green willow rods are inserted in moist, loamy ground over the winter, where they will begin to send out roots. They can then be woven together into decorative forms; in the spring, the branches will leaf out and transform the piece into a living sculpture.

Left: This bench is sheltered by a wicker half-dome that, because it is so light, is easy to move and set up in any part of the garden. **Right:** Willow canes can be easily molded to create a cozy nook in the garden. Here, shaped to form a leafy bower arching over two rustic log chairs, they make up a frame sturdy enough to hold a string of lights in the summer, transforming the green arch into a vault of stars.

Wrought Iron

Usually reserved for public structures like pavilions or kiosks, wrought iron can also be used to build small, light structures to cover a bench or armchair. Thin metal rods can make a structure that becomes practically invisible when painted green, but is strong enough to support climbing plants. When not covered in vegetation, the metal may seem a little out of place in the garden, but garlanded with flowering vines, it fades into the background and lets the form of the climbing plants shine. The simplest designs are arches available at garden stores, often in kits that you can put together yourself. It is important to secure the structure solidly to the ground before you let plants clamber over it to make a leafy shelter, under which you can place a chair or a bench. More sophisticated and costly, custom-made structures

can fit a variety of purposes, such as to cover a seating area set against a bank or the side of a house. When you choose climbing plants, keep in mind how much weight your framework can bear and how much shade you would like. Slow-growing species like large-flowered clematis, or fast-growing annuals such as sweet peas, morning glories, or scarlet runner bean, will cast a light shade without overloading the metal structure. On the other hand, more vigorous plants, such as honeysuckle or wisteria, can quickly overrun the frame, possibly damaging it as well as making the space below too gloomy.

Facing page and above: This custom-made wrought-iron framework, partly anchored in the mortar of a stone banquette, offers support to climbing plants and shelter to those using this sanctuary nestled into the side of a hill. The banquette below, which echoes the wrought iron's curving shape, is strewn with soft cushions that transform this shelter into a luxurious retreat.

Ornamental Wood

Although similar to pergolas or arbors, from which they take inspiration, these wooden shelters have one difference: their size. Rather than a table or an entire garden room, they are designed to accommodate a bench or two chairs, covering barely twenty square feet of space. Often set against a hedge or placed at the end of a garden walk, these smaller structures may also be found along a pathway or set into a flower border. The basic design is created with posts that hold up two long, parallel beams, which are in turn connected with a regular succession of rafters, like the series of arches that creates a tunnel over a covered walkway. Larger versions may take some elements from the pergola, such as massive square posts or trellised panels, but they are still only deep enough to shelter a bench or two chairs side by side. Though climbing plants might effectively ornament smaller, simpler versions, most of these wooden structures look better left free of obscuring foliage so that their elegant design, their pleasing proportions, and their fine workmanship, often with mortise and tenon joints, can be fully appreciated.

A WORD OF ADVICE

It is possible to turn a standard square pergola made from a kit, originally designed to shade a table and chairs, into an intimate seating nook by simply shortening the cross beams while leaving the long beams the same length. The resulting shallow rectangle will be ideal to shelter a bench or two chairs, and easier to fit into a garden with limited space.

Facing page, left: Inspired by an arbor, this basic rest shelter uses a simple structure of posts and a few pieces of trellis to create an alcove of greenery around a stone bench. **Facing page, right:** Set into a mixed border, this trellised wooden shelter, tucked away at a bend in the pathway and almost obscured by lush vegetation, conveys an enchanting air of mystery. **Above:** The elegant form of this pastel-painted wooden structure is too charming to be obscured by climbing plants: it is nicely set off, on the other hand, by the soft masses of ornamental grass and flowering perennials around it.

The Little Cabana

These carefully crafted small structures, typical of English gardens, are the most elaborate rest shelters; some are even real little cabins, with only the front left completely open. These miniature cabanas can be distinguished from leafy bowers or truncated pergolas by the fact that they have solid roofs, making them effective shelters against inclement weather. Their compact design makes them easy to accommodate in any part of the garden, though they are most effective when set into a hedge that is partly cut away to fit around them, saving space that might be needed for walks or flower beds. Such gazebos can almost disappear in the surrounding greenery, creating a private place to sit and look out over the garden. They usually contain either a freestanding bench or a built-in banquette that faces the garden or the surrounding countryside—for these little shelters can also be set up in more open areas. Their design should reflect the style of the garden. If the garden is chic and refined, such a cabana might boast ornamental details and a decorative trellis; in a garden with a more rural style, it might be built of rustic materials and left essentially unadorned.

Above: Even through the mantle of greenery, the finely crafted architectural details can still be seen in this little cabana. Harmonious proportions, delicate decorative trelliswork, and an elegant checkered flooring combine to create a graceful and comfortable shelter.

Top: A bench can be integrated into a framework of subtle architecture, like here, where the graceful ogive of the roof evokes the hull of an overturned boat. **Above, left:** Rustic but chic, this A-frame cabana clothed in larch shingles shelters a bench constructed of exotic wood; a large opening flanked by two tall windows offers views onto the garden. **Above, right:** Resembling a hut with a thatched roof, this bucolic-looking log cabana houses a long banquette set on a platform, allowing the resting visitor to look down over the surroundings from a little height.

Tents and Awnings

These light, temporary structures can be set up in the garden during summer to protect large tables and outdoor entertainment areas from the heat of the sun. Attached to the low branches of a tree, suspended from ropes, or stretched between poles driven into the ground, these shelters are the "featherweights" of garden architecture and have a nomadic quality, set up on the spur of the moment as we move around in the garden. But cloth panels do more than tame the sun's rays and offer a little cool shade; they also flutter in the breeze. One of the magical effects of these soft curtains is the ephemeral play of light and shadow they bring to their surroundings as they move in a soft breath of air—an ever-changing spectacle that can be enhanced, as night falls, by the flickering light of lamps and candles.

In this nomadic, ephemeral shelter, chestnut trellises and bundles of branches from a seasonal pruning are topped with light, translucent row-cover fabric, of the kind sold in garden centers for frost or insect protection. Moved by the softest breezes, this fleeting decoration will delight children during a garden or birthday party.

Drapes and Veils

Like the tents we set up when camping, temporary shelters made of cloth panels can be erected and dismantled as we desire. Until recently, only mosquito netting and sturdy canvas could last long outside in all kinds of weather, but innovations in durability mean that many modern fabrics can be used in the garden without having to be brought in every time there is a light shower. On the other hand, the ordinary linen and cotton cloth—the sheets and tablecloths of our grandparents—that we find at flea markets and in our attics can be reasonably durable, if it is fairly heavy. Use in the garden as hangings is hardly a challenge to these fabrics' sturdiness, and they make effective materials for a garden tent. But the most useful resource is net curtains—whether synthetic or cotton—converted from their original use for garden shelters. Another approach is to buy new, inexpensive sheets at a large department store; they will only last one season, but that takes care of the winter storage problem. To make wall panels or roofs with them, simply attach them to the low branches of a tree or on cords suspended between two trunks. If there is no natural support, you can also build a structure out of bamboo canes or chestnut poles.

Left: Traditional mosquito netting is draped from a branch like a tent, forming an intimate space that offers protection from the wind and insects, but not from the eyes of others. **Right:** Generous expanses of fabric stiffened with a framework of wooden or metal poles and hung from the branches of a tree or from iron rods make a temporary wall that blocks the wind and creates a private area.

Canopies and Awnings

Forget the traditional umbrella, which is too small to shade a reasonable area and seems to fall over at the slightest breeze; we want proper canopies and awnings. These cloth panels, suspended at their peak from solidly anchored poles and stretched taut by cables running to the ground, are much closer in spirit to a Berber tent than to a wooden garden house. They are, however, much in vogue, and well loved for the protection they give from the sun's rays. Modern synthetic materials impermeable to water can even shelter you from the rain, making them even more popular. These fabrics can be used in all kinds of ways, on terraces and patios as well as in the garden. Equipped with grommets, they are traditionally attached to poles, but can also be anchored to the side of a building or a tree trunk, or suspended from cables. The slope of the canvas depends on the height of the poles or points of attachment, and itself produces undulations in the fabric. The chief drawback of this kind of suspended canvas shelter is that it has no walls, and therefore lacks intimacy. Hanging some fabric to close up the sides, or installing wooden side panels, will give more privacy to the structure.

Above, left: A canopy attached to poles is stabilized by ropes that, anchored to the ground, stretch the canvas tight. In this sun-drenched landscape, the fabric casts a refreshing light shade without cluttering up the space or blocking the view. **Above, right:** Suspending a triangle of canvas from the high branch of a neighboring tree creates a steeply angled canopy, which better protects those underneath from the rays of the sun. The shadows of the foliage above create a dramatic, ever-changing show.

Movable Shelters

Caravans have accommodated the good life on the road for many years, and some have now been retired, to be installed in gardens for a well-earned rest. These period pieces and authentic copies come at quite a price, but the cleverest among us know how to get around that: build one yourself. A caravan is not the only light, movable shelter one can have in the garden, though: both yurts and Berber tents have made a recent appearance. Whether this represents a fleeting fad or genuine appreciation for these small mobile structures, bohemian habitats have always offered an alternative to traditional garden structures.

These days, the traditional caravan is quite sought after to create a garden retreat—more than just a garden shed, it can serve as a true supplementary dwelling. Since the caravan has wheels, no permit is needed to install it.

The Caravan

What could be more natural than the wish to intall a horse-drawn caravan—symbolic as it is of freedom and the charm of the bohemian life—as a mobile dwelling in the garden? But authentic caravans are hard to come by, and reproductions are expensive. So why not set out to build one? No need to be an expert at bodywork; these wagons are made of wood, and only the wheels and the chassis have anything to do with mechanical function. Just remember, a caravan is nothing but a shed on wheels; it is easy to create the illusion of one by building, for example, a shed on top of a hay wagon or flatbed trailer, or to adapt one from a construction trailer. Even more simply, you might customize a modest garden shed by equipping it with a few accessories that are characteristic of a caravan. First, raise it on cinder blocks; then, attach wooden circles to represent wheels—or better yet, attach real wheels found in a junkyard. Then replace the flat or A-frame roof with a rounded one, paint the walls with bright colors, and all that's left is to attach some stairs straight up to the doors to perfect the illusion. To really set the stage, opt for a bohemian style of decoration, collecting containers of all kinds in which to plant old-fashioned cottage-garden flowers—hollyhocks, marigolds, and sunflowers—and heighten the mystery by covering your caravan with exuberant vegetation.

Above: This gypsy wagon is a large garden shed on wheels, spacious and comfortable enough to serve as guest quarters when space in the house gets tight. Often more luxuriously fitted out than a camper, it is more elegant and easier to integrate into the garden.

The Nomadic Tent

Although they are sometimes imported from North Africa, Bedouin and Berber tents are very hard to find; a few rental companies offer them as theme party props. These sturdy canvas shelters guarantee the ultimate in exotic atmosphere when they are set up in the garden—if, of course, they are set in a suitable environment, with appropriate plantings. Sand dunes, reeds, and palms are indispensable to complete the tableau—which must also be temporary, because the material used in genuine nomadic tents does not hold up to rainy weather very well. It might be better, then, to create something inspired by these structures, using fabric better adapted to a cold, wet climate, or even to think of another kind of portable shelter, such as a tepee or yurt.

Top: A makeshift shelter to last a summer: halfway between a tepee and a yurt, this tent is made from a structure of poles driven into the ground in a circle, tied together at the top, and then draped with heavy row-cover fabric. **Above:** A real Berber tent creates a quiet, intimate atmosphere, but cannot be left outside long in inclement weather.

The Yurt

These felt-covered wood-lattice-framed structures are the stereotypical Mongol dwelling. Light and mobile, yurts can be raised and taken down in no time, but are perfectly habitable and comfortable despite their provisional quality. The structures are all from the same design and made from the same pattern, which offers a lot of interior space. The wooden frame is made of vertical trellised walls that are held in place by compressing bands (in modern yurts, a tension cable), and support a succession of slats that form a rounded top with a central opening. The whole thing is covered by layers of insulating wool felt, sandwiched between two sheets of canvas, the exterior one treated to make it weatherproof. Inside, a wood floor insulates the space from the ground, making the yurt perfectly habitable and comfortable. For this reason, this type of structure is becoming more popular, and not just as an eccentric shed; in fact, the yurt is becoming a "green" living choice as a main residence, with an ever more comfortable and stylish interior. Some companies have begun to sell yurts in kits, so they are becoming even more accessible.

A WORD OF ADVICE

Since its introduction to America in 1962, the yurt as a "green" housing choice has exploded in popularity. Many companies now offer yurt kits for sale, some simple and portable, others of high-tech materials and design and not at all easy to dismantle and move. Even though most yurts are easily dismantled, they may still require a building permit, so be sure to check for local regulations and restrictions, especially if you plan to use your yurt as a primary residence. Some manufactured yurts are designed to conform to the Uniform Building Code regarding structural load requirements, so they may be erected as permanent structures even where they are subject to building code standards.

Facing page: The yurts seen here—quite hard-to-find examples, as very few are exported—are authentic original designs created by hand in Kazakhstan and Turkmenistan, as can be seen in the details of their wooden framework. But the yurt has been a victim of its own success: more and more yurts are being manufactured in Europe and America, often resembling the original only in name.

Greenhouses and Conservatories

A greenhouse is a garden shed in which the wooden wall and roofing have been replaced with glass panes. An indispensable tool for the serious gardener, allowing the propagation, cultivation, and protection of tender plants, the greenhouse is a work of art no matter its size or the materials used. The simplest form is made with a frame of metal or wood, with a floor space of only twenty or thirty square feet. Easily adapted to fit in small gardens, a greenhouse can be attached to a wall to take up as little space as possible. More sophisticated models have a complex, often decorative frame that may enclose several hundred square feet. Designed originally for starting vegetables and fruits early or over-wintering tender plants, some greenhouses have been transformed into conservatories, sheltering collections of rare plants. With the addition of furniture, a greenhouse can be turned into an extra room for relaxing or pottering, although the glass overhead does not offer protection from the sun.

The glass panes of this classic old greenhouse, situated against a south-facing wall to better retain heat, are set into its curving panels to create a very attractive "fish-scale" effect.

The Wood-Framed Greenhouse

Antique greenhouses with wooden frames are rare, since they are quite vulnerable to water damage and therefore do not have a long lifespan. Original examples from the early days of the wood-framed greenhouse have all but disappeared, which is not to say that one should not use wood today, especially since it can be cheaper than a metal frame. All the same, wood, even if it is treated appropriately, is still affected by humidity; and in a greenhouse humidity is a constant that one can do nothing about. Water evaporates naturally from the leaves of plants, and a high rate of humidity is often deliberately maintained, especially for plants originally from the tropics. It is thus difficult to stop dampness from attacking a wooden frame. In addition, a wooden greenhouse needs a thicker framework than a metal greenhouse. The larger the greenhouse, the more weight the framework must support, making it necessary to use interior pillars and heavy braces to hold up the roof. As well as diminishing the light, this gives the greenhouse a heavier, less elegant look.

A WORD OF ADVICE

If you are interested in building a greenhouse, make sure to orient it according to its intended purpose. If you are going to use it for horticultural reasons—that is, for propagating and cultivating fruits, vegetables, and flowers—place it so it faces south or southwest, to receive the most light and warmth from the sun. On the other hand, if you want it to be a place to relax in, or to use as an extra living space, a southern exposure will make the inside too hot and uncomfortable. Better to give it a view of the sunrise or sunset by orienting it toward the northeast or northwest.

Facing page, top: A wood-framed roof makes for a rather bulky structure, as the wood frame needs to be quite large to support the weight of the glass, but this naturally insulating material also reduces thermal transfer between the interior and exterior of a greenhouse. **Facing page, bottom:** One solution to the bulkiness of wood is mixed construction: this greenhouse's wood-framed sides are topped by a lighter steel-framed glass roof, giving it a sleeker, more elegant look. However, the combination of two materials that respond differently to changes in weather may adversely effect both the water- and airtightness of the building and its efficiency in retaining heat.

The Steel-Framed Greenhouse

The monumental greenhouses in public botanical gardens are by necessity constructed of steel, the only material strong enough to support the weight of these glass cathedrals. But steel is also popular for building small, stylish structures in private gardens. Though the size may vary, these almost always follow the same basic plan: a lean-to or free-standing structure with a square or rectangular footprint, and glass sides that can curve toward the roof or meet it at an angle. The only difference is in the ornamentation and the accessories—doors, shelves, roll-up shades, automatic or manual vents—depending on the greenhouse's purpose and the financial means of its owners. Some of the greenhouses saved from oblivion by careful historical restoration are veritable jewels of architecture, demonstrating a technical and aesthetic prowess that brings them great esteem. While the restoration and maintenance

of a traditional steel-framed greenhouse is a lot of work, today's greenhouses are built using improved techniques and materials. Aluminum—much lighter and more resistant to humidity, and requiring little upkeep—is replacing steel; and polycarbonate glazing, a transparent material that is sturdy and insulating, and comes in double- and triple-wall construction for higher efficiency, has taken the place of glass panes. The look of contemporary greenhouses may not have changed, but the comfort of their interiors and their ease of maintenance have been greatly improved. Greenhouses today are often charming spaces for relaxation and entertainment, fitted out with lounge furniture and luxury features such as pools and spas. In gardens, they've reached a new level of sophistication, equaling the most elegant gazebos and loggias, while offering their users an intimate contact with nature.

Facing page: Modern greenhouses use new materials like aluminum frames and double-walled polycarbonate glazing with a UV-protective layer that reduces the impact of the sun and controls the temperature of the interior. But they are still finely crafted buildings that conserve the look of greenhouses of yesterday. **Above:** Metal frames can have a delicate and graceful form. Only glass can be used to follow the curved lines of this building as newer, more insulating materials would not be flexible enough.

Shelters for Birds

Those who enjoy the garden are many, and we must count the birds among their number. Whether in the country or in town, birds make the garden their own, setting up house or finding temporary shelter. You can attract birds by planting fruit-bearing shrubs and letting flowers go to seed, but once they have come, you must take care of them. Birds are invaluable garden helpers, devouring a number of parasitic insects—a couple of tits can protect an orchard of about forty trees, for example—and creating an enchanting atmosphere with their song. To benefit from their services and sounds, make it easy for them by installing birdhouses and feeders to invite them to make themselves at home in the garden. These easty-to-make structures are nothing more than small garden sheds!

Decorative elements in their own right, birdhouses are also a clever way to invite birds into the garden. Ready-made models are often preferable, since their dimensions and the diameter of their entrance holes have been fashioned to suit specific species.

Birdhouses

Our environment is becoming less and less hospitable for birds, who struggle to find lodging. Hollow trees are rare in developed areas, and modern buildings with their smooth and uniform facades, especially in an urban setting, offer few nooks and crannies to receive nests or offer perches. Yet many of our best-loved species, like the chickadee, are hole-nesting birds. One of the best ways to stem the decline of the avian population in our gardens is by installing nest boxes. Though it doesn't matter too much what they look like, their dimensions—especially that of the entrance hole—cannot be left to chance. A diameter between one and one and a half inches will allow the desired bird species to enter while discouraging their competitors. There are many types of birdhouses recommended by the Audubon Society and offered in stores, and these are guaranteed to attract birds reasonably well. Use these as models when making your own birdhouses, and be wary of overly artistic shelters that, because they are too large or too light, will remain depressingly empty. Don't be surprised to find that a simple mailbox can easily satisfy a bird's desire for nesting. Be sure to supplement these lodgings with berry bushes and some prickly shrubs that give protection from predators. A hedge, for example, with a number of dense and forked branches, offers a great place for a nest. And be sure not to bother these nests, from the end of March to mid-July, by trimming hedges or coming too close.

Above, left: Exotic birdhouses are fun structures that can be a nice addition to garden decor, but they don't always suit the birds' needs. Use different types of nest boxes around the garden to improve your chances of attracting a variety of birds. **Above, right:** Even if it is perched six feet above the ground, a birdhouse on a tripod still offers easy prey for cats. Keep your bases to a simple single pole; a wide baffle will add extra protection from climbing predators.

A WORD OF ADVICE

Birdhouses and their contents attract a number of predators—not only cats, but many other small animals that live in the garden. A narrow entrance hole makes it hard for uninvited intruders to get in, and you can even buy nest boxes especially equipped with interior flaps that impede an inquisitive paw. But it is better to simply keep the birdhouse difficult to reach. Attaching it to a flat wall or the trunk of a tree that has been high-pruned discourages most felines. Suspending it from a chain or cord is also an excellent way to keep it out of reach, but not all birds appreciate the way such suspended shelters sway. Finally, face the opening away from the prevailing wind and rain, and opt for hardwood rather than particleboard, as it is much more weather resistant.

Above: The lack of proper walls leaves this birdhouse exposed to bad weather and to the view of predators; shelters of this type, though quite decorative, are better used as bird feeders rather than nest boxes.

Bird Feeders

Though experts do not agree on whether feeding birds is good for them or creates a detrimental dependence, the fact remains that it attracts them to the garden and helps them survive through periods of severe cold. As with birdhouses, bird feeders and their environs are favorite hunting zones for predators. Perch them up high and out in the open, to give the birds time to see coming danger and fly away. Here as well, there are numerous styles, and bird feeders offer a little more scope for the imagination than do birdhouses. Platform feeders have an open tray that offers easy access, but also exposes the feed to rain that may foster mold, adding to the risk of disease. Enclosed hopper and tube feeders with perches keep seed dry and dispense it evenly—but access is often limited to only one or two birds at a time. Finally, hanging mesh feeders can be used only by those acrobatic birds, like nuthatches and titmice, who are able to cling to the frame while eating. As for the feed, some popular choices are seeds—sunflower, oats, melon, safflower, and pumpkin—suet cakes, and fruits, even overripe ones. Avoid dry bread and salty foods, which can make birds too thirsty, especially during a freeze, when water can be scarce. Place the feeders in various parts of the garden, near enough to the house so that you are able to watch the birds' activities, but far away enough so that they may eat in peace.

Above, left: Raised on a post, this feeder assures tranquility and security for the birds while they eat and allows them to be easily observed.
Above, right: Feeders give the imagination a freer rein than birdhouses. However, the bird food should be sheltered from bad weather, and the feeding platform should be out in the open, so that the birds have time to fly away in case of danger. **Facing page:** Dried fruits—and even walnuts and hazelnuts—are appreciated by birds like the blue tit, who also eats insects and is one of the few species who can cling to the wire of the feeder while eating.

Dovecotes and Aviaries

Aviaries designed for chickens, turtledoves, and domesticated pigeons combine a solid shelter and an open space, enclosed by chicken wire or simple mesh. When the garden is small, the shelter is usually attached to a fenced-in run, while in a large garden, it is positioned inside a large cage. The style and refinement of the aviary or shelter depend on the type of bird that it houses. In effect, those interested in hens only for their eggs can meet their needs with a rough and functional structure, often relegated to the back of the garden. On the other hand, a collection of prize bantams or turtledoves merits some-thing more attractive and sophisticated. The shelter can be enriched with embellishments that make it a decorative element in the garden, enhanced with well-chosen plants. A planted area, however, is not always compatible with the presence and appetites of birds, who often leave a barren landscape in their wake, where only inanimate ornamentation can survive!

A dovecote is a building big enough to house pigeons and turtledoves raised in a natural habitat. The largest versions are proper buildings that allow the birds' owners not only to care for them but to observe them. These buildings, used by pigeon associations, private collectors, or societies, require constant watch and regular attention. The smallest versions are more appropriate for housing a couple of birds and as a graceful ornament to the garden.

Facing page: Dovecotes in private gardens are more substantial in form than birdhouses, and shelter one couple or more of pigeons or turtledoves that can move about freely. **Above:** A veritable miniature opera house! Combining a sheltered space, green landscaping, and decorative elements, this aviary inhabited and animated by its flock of doves, which can fly around in an enclosed space that prevents them from escaping while protecting them from predators.

Shelters for Insects

Insects are indispensable to the ecosystem of our gardens, and encouraging them to thrive contributes to the ecological balance of the area. To achieve this, we must offer them lodging: a well-manicured modern garden may lack the natural cavities—such as the trunks of dead trees, layers of leaves or moss, or crevices in stones—insects need for refuge from the elements in summer and winter, protection from predators, and space for their nests. The human urge to keep the garden neat, aseptic, weeded, and cleaned of all waste often deprives insects of their natural habitats. To make up for this, it is necessary to create shelters for insects that, more than just housing them, encourage the development of colonies of those species that are useful for fighting parasitic insects. These beneficial insects are essential soldiers in the biological battle.

Deadwood deliberately left in a hedge, or in a corner of the garden, can provide a home for useful insects, such as bees and solitary wasps, who would normally find homes in the holes left by the larvae of wood-boring insects.

Nests and Hiding Places

The easiest way to re-create a natural biotope for microfauna is to let a corner of the garden go wild. Allowing the close-cut lawn to grow long like a meadow, leaving a hedge to grow bushy, not weeding, and not picking up leaves and fallen branches are some of the easy-to-apply principles for reconstructing a well-balanced environment. However, in a small garden, it is not always possible to leave an area to go wild. Another way to offer lodging, especially to beneficial insects, is the use of artificial shelters. Most insects seek out small crevices, such as the hollow stems of grasses, bamboo, umbellifers such as angelica or Queen Anne's lace, or hollow-stalked shrubs such as elder. They also like the holes left by the larvae of boring insects in deadwood, which you can re-create by drilling holes between one-sixteenth and one-half inch in diameter in a section of a trunk, a log, or a dried-out branch, being careful to drill only into the wood and not completely through it. You can also cut hollow stalks—about eight inches long—and group them in bundles of about fifteen or twenty. Place these little shelters in various spots around the garden, up to six feet off the ground.

Above: An original sculpture that also serves as an insect shelter is both pleasant to look at and useful. Here, a globe made out of a series of wire circles mimics an aquarium; around its base are twined yards of woody stems, ideal habitat for beneficial insects.

Top, left: The hollow stalks of umbellifers quickly deteriorate in bad weather, but set into a wooden box placed in the lee of prevailing winds and driving rain, they make durable homes for insects. **Top, right:** A collection of logs with holes drilled in them and bundles of hollow stalks, arranged on some old shelves or under the eaves of a shed, creates an original decoration and a veritable insect hotel. **Bottom, left:** For drilled logs, choose dense wood like oak, hornbeam, chestnut, or beech rather than the soft wood of conifers, whose fibers expand when damp. Cover the log with a roof to protect it from rain. **Bottom, right:** Earwigs suffer from a bad reputation, though they can eat a large quantity of aphids in just one night. During the day, they take refuge in the cool shade under pots filled with straw and suspended on stakes, in light contact with foliage.

Gazebos

Gazebos are garden shelters with open sides, rather than walls, interrupted only by the posts that support the roofing. Sometimes found in private gardens, but more commonly seen in public parks, these little works of art, whether circular, square, or hexagonal, are both decorative features and shelters. Some models don't have a solid roof but, rather like pergolas, are topped with a metal or wooden framework meant to be covered with climbing plants, whose foliage more or less hides the structure—offering a privacy quite sought after, of old, for romantic interludes.

Open-Roofed Gazebos

These shelters open to the sky, so popular in nineteenth-century gardens, make an attractive destination for a garden stroll and a decorative place to sit and admire the landscape. Open-roofed gazebos, inspired by the leafy bowers found in Renaissance gardens, can be distinguished from them by their solid and durable framework, which provides ample support to climbing plants. These jewels of garden architecture are placed at strategic points in the garden, well in view of the residence or at the axis of a perspective. They are most effectively positioned not only where they ornament the view themselves but also offer a commanding perspective over the grounds and, if they are raised on a promontory like a belvedere, even the surrounding countryside. Since they lack a solid roof, however, these gazebos offer shelter from the sun but not from the rain, so they can be enjoyed only in fair weather.

Open-roofed gazebos have a transparency of form that allows them to blend into the garden discreetly but some styles stand out more boldly than others. Those clothed in lattice or trellis sections, for instance, make the walls and roof more visible against the greenery.

Above: A gravel path passes through an elegant octagonal gazebo, whose framework is covered in lattice panels and whose pastel blue color enhances the romantic effect of the decor. **Facing page:** Swathed in a mantle of foliage and flowers, the structure of this gazebo is reduced to its most basic expression. With no trellis and a roof in name only, the shape of this shelter is outlined with pillars and simple framework and decorated only with a few wood arabesques.

The Classical Gazebo

Whether they overlooked the gardens of the Italian Renaissance, the geometric French parterres, or the Romantic English landscape, the style of gazebos has remained unchanged. Built on a hexagonal base, these wooden structures are covered in trellis or ornamental openwork that gives them a refined but very classical look. Some versions are enhanced with flourishes carved in wood, such as vases, arabesques, and trompe-l'oeil decorations. Classical gazebos should be exposed to full view, not too obscured by climbing plants, because their value as works of garden art lies in the way they punctuate the sight lines of garden allées and the vistas they provide. Once inside them, one can appreciate the delicacy of their structure, the precision of their craftsmanship, and above all, their value as a retreat sheltered from the sun. Today, however, it is quite rare to come across an authentic antique gazebo, since the wood used to build them has often not stood the test of time. However, faithful reproductions of these historic structures exist, and these have the added benefit of being made with treated lumber. The most affordable versions are made from do-it-yourself kits sold by garden companies; though their look imitates that of the gracious gazebos of old, their finish betrays their standardized production.

A WORD OF ADVICE

For custom-made models, choose hard wood that is naturally resistant to damp weather, such as acacia, oak, or chestnut; wood available locally will be less expensive than exotic wood, which must be shipped long distances. Standard models are most often made of pressure-treated white pine from managed forests. Though much cheaper, these are not the best choice for the environment.

The Pergola-Roofed Gazebo

This type of garden shelter, though it sits like a gazebo on a square, hexagonal, or octagonal base, has a flat top like that of a pergola rather than a conical or domed top. It usually straddles a garden walkway, or is placed to take advantage of a view. Though its roof is flat, a flourishing mound of vines growing over such a structure can give the illusion of the dome that tops a traditional gazebo. This has the advantage of reducing the cost of the structure as well as simplifying its construction, especially if you are building it yourself. To reinforce this likeness to a gazebo and escape the no-frills look of a pergola, simply add the typical gazebo details such as ornamental brackets that link the pillars to the roof beams or trellised side panels. Finally, the choice of climbing plants plays an important role: this is a good place for vigorous and luxuriant species, such as climbing roses, honeysuckle, or wisteria, as long as the structure can support their weight.

Facing page and above: Drowned under climbing roses such as 'Albéric Barbier,' 'Seagull,' and 'Bobbie James,' a mass of foliage and flowers conceals the flat roof of these shelters, forming a green dome that creates the illusion of a raised roof.

A New Take on the Classical Gazebo

Gazebo styles have kept pace with the evolution of garden design; the classical structures that adorned the parks of the eighteenth and nineteenth centuries gave way to more modern structures that none-theless retained the appearance of the age-old gazebos. Today's structures, whether built on a round, square, or hexagonal base, offer a pure, clean outline devoid of all superfluous accessories. What remains is a wood or iron structure reduced to its most elemental form, but still clearly sketching the form of a gazebo. When the structure does include decorative ornaments, they consist merely of a fac-ing of vertical lattice or iron rods. Modern materials and construction techniques have also influenced this sober look, which reflects the minimalist style of the gardens of the twentieth century. The use of laminated wood, galvanized steel, and aluminum, and new techniques for bending metal and wood or cutting them with the use of a computer, have also opened new avenues for both artisans and garden designers. For an overview, take some walks in a few public parks and gardens, which are usually filled with these modern garden structures.

Above: Vertical wood laths give this octagonal gazebo a resolutely modern look while allowing a classical shape to show through. **Facing page:** Halfway between a domed aviary and a gazebo, this building has the overall form of a classical gazebo, but its widely spaced arches and circles of clean, bare wood give it a contemporary air.

The Modern Gazebo

Contemporary gazebos have little in common with traditional versions, other than in name and general principle. Yes, these structures are made of wood with open sides, but there the comparison ends, since the style, the combination of materials, and the construction techniques have more in common with modern architecture than with the historical gazebo. Suited to modern gardens with their sober lines, contemporary gazebos distinguish themselves by their airy look and their clean design. To appear as light as possible and to blend into the environment, they use a minimum of supporting pillars—two, three, or four—though these may be quite monumental, as are the master beams that support the roof frame. The overhead structure can be of wood, arranged geometrically like a contemporary trellis, but more often today it traces curved lines that evoke the wing of a bird. This type of roof calls for bold

modern materials—steel, laminates, and canvas—to achieve its futuristic and innovative look. Such a roof emphasizes the steel cables used to shape and stabilize the roofing, rather than supporting it from underneath, with solid braces between the roof and the side columns. Here, instead, the roof is suspended from cables stretched from the top of high pillars, so that it appears to be hanging in midair. This method frees up the interior space to become a true living area. Open to all sides—though it can be closed off with sliding panels or curtains—this modern gazebo is often equipped with furniture built into the structure itself. A wide shelf around the inside of the structure outlines its form, but also acts as a bench, settee, or coffee table.

Facing page and above: This cube-shaped modern gazebo, set at one end of a canal that cuts through the garden, revives the spirit of the Moorish pavilions. With its roomy wooden benches under the striped shade of its roofing, the gazebo can't help but evoke Morocco, proving once again that modernity is nothing but the reinterpretation and realization of ancient principles.

The Wrought-Steel Gazebo

Steel-framed gazebos differ from wooden structures in their delicate form, which becomes practically invisible when the structure is painted a subtle color or covered in vegetation. The strength of tubular forged steel allows the creation of a tough and impressive framework that can easily support the weight of exuberant climbing plants. Traditional steel gazebos have always been created on the same plan, whether round, square, or hexagonal: corner pilasters made of two or three vertical bars of steel, bound together by horizontal rods. These pilasters in turn support a roof, whose shape can enhance the style of the piece, since the steel can be bent to create any shape. Some models are equipped with trellised side panels, through which climbing plants can weave, giving the structure an intimate interior. These structures resemble little summerhouses, with closed walls and only one point of entry.

A WORD OF ADVICE

At one time wrought iron needed many coats of paint to resist rust in bad weather. Metal structures, regardless of how well they were maintained, did not last a long time. Today, galvanizing techniques and plastic coatings, such as enamel epoxies, protect the surface of steel or iron so that it does not need to be repainted over and over again.

Above, left: The metal framework of a gazebo made of steel rods creates a strong but light structure that will blend discreetly with its environment if it is painted in a dark color. **Above, right, and facing page:** Gazebos with trellised walls and climbing plants create an intimate enclosed space similar to a little summerhouse.

The Fanciful Gazebo

Gazebos can be insipired works of architecture or garden art. They can be custom made to capture the atmosphere of parks of the nineteenth century, or the architecture of faraway countries, such as Chinese pagodas with their upswept roofing. These original and unique pieces should not be hidden under a thick mantle of foliage or flowers, but are best seen free of all vegetation to show off their striking form and ornamentation. Installed on a promontory in a park or at the intersection of two walkways in a small garden, these architectural fantasies merit considerable thought in their placement, not only to be seen themselves, but also so that their occupants can admire the scenery. An isolated position far from the house and from the more frequented parts of the garden makes them perfect for meditation and for daydreaming.

Above: This Asian-inspired gazebo, combining a carefully crafted wooden frame with an overhead screen of steel tubes, sits enthroned in the heart of a garden composed with oriental species such as magnolia, Japanese azaleas, and rhododendrons.

The Rotunda

The bandstands typical of nineteenth-century urban squares are probably the largest rotundas still in existence. With their round bases and open sides, with or without solid roofs, they were designed to house brass bands and orchestras and thus took on grand proportions. Impractical for small gardens, these structures can still serve as a source of inspiration for green rotundas that, as their name implies, are constructed with a round base enhanced with pilasters or posts supporting various styles of roof. A flat framework covered in climbing plants, as in a pergola, is easier to build than a vaulted arch, cupola, or curved pagoda-style roof, more complex and decorative forms that look better when left free of vegetation. The circular form of this shelter gives it a friendly feel, and the absence of any angles promotes an atmosphere of peace and serenity. The rotunda is most often used as an open-roofed room, close to the house, where one can enjoy meals al fresco.

Above: Backed up by trellised panels and buried under clusters of wisteria blossoms, this flowery rotunda adjacent to a terrace makes for a valuable shady refuge during the hot part of the day. **Left:** With its low wall supporting a metallic framework for grape vines to clamber over, this green rotunda blends so nicely into its surroundings that one forgets its ample size and paved floor.

Covered Gazebos

Unlike open-air gazebos, these shelters are equipped with roofs that make them much more adaptable to a variety of functions. Outfitted with comfortable furniture that transforms them into extra rooms, they can welcome people to the garden in all temperatures. Because we are not forced to flee them in case of rain, covered gazebos can be placed in secluded parts of the garden, far from the house. They thus become boudoirs to retire to when seeking calm, serenity, and a little intimacy, while at the same time staying in contact with the nature around us. Unlike a garden shed, they have no walls, so they allow complete immersion in the garden and its secrets.

Enclosed with a finely crafted balustrade, this octagonal gazebo has a refined quality that extends up to a roof edged with a decorative band of shingles. The roof is crowned with a miniature gazebo that echoes the geometric form of the larger structure.

The Grand Gazebo

Ever-more-spacious garden gazebos bear witness to the increasingly popular pastime of living in the open air. Even the most basic models have space for garden furniture, while the more luxurious are outfitted with outdoor kitchens, bars, or even Jacuzzis. Some combine space heaters with removable heavy canvas walls or trellised panels to close up the space, so that it can be used from spring to fall. A step down from custom-made models, mass-produced large-scale models are simpler in design. Only in the shape of the roof, most often a four-sided pyramid, do these retain the look of the traditional gazebo; their columns and framework tend to be very plain. For these structures, the role of vegetation is important, softening the mass-produced look by hiding the columns and the perimeter of the roof under garlands of foliage and flowers. Vigorous clematis species or annual climbers are your best bet, since their twining vines produce a decorative effect quickly and they are easily controlled by pruning, to keep the sides open and preserve a clear view of the garden. To make your gazebo more comfortable, add vertical blinds or sections of trellis as protection against prevailing winds and drafts. Laying down a raised wooden floor creates an insulating space under the floor to block damp rising from the ground, making the space more comfortable after showers or on a rainy day.

Facing page: The structure of this gazebo set against a hedge is partly obscured by climbing plants, creating a green grotto and hiding the posts, so that the elegant Asian-inspired roof seems to float above the vegetation. **Above:** The refined quality of the composition, the care given to the decor, and the charm of the furniture soften the rustic quality of this gazebo, planted in the heart of the woods, and invite relaxation and contemplation.

The Rustic Gazebo

The style and materials used for this gazebo reflect the surrounding countryside. In a wooded area or in a country garden, rustic materials and less elaborate construction will better suit the setting and allow for more imperfections. For the uprights and the roof frame, the unstripped logs used as posts and the rough beams that frame the ceiling make a harmonious whole. The use of logs and branches of irregular sizes and shapes, salvaged from pruning, also adds to the rural spirit, evoking the fanciful rocaille style of the late eighteenth century. Roof shingles of larch or fir crown the work, enhancing the country atmosphere. After a few years, the patina of the wood will deepen the effect, allowing the structure to blend into the landscape as if it had always been there.

Above: Installed at the edge of a wood, this hexagonal gazebo, its floor covered with salvaged cobblestones, displays a country style underlined by the use of unstripped fir posts and a roof covered in larch shingles.

The Romantic Gazebo

Both the choice of materials and the elaborate construction of the framework are vital to the style of this gazebo. To affirm the romantic spirit, the materials were carefully crafted and assembled, including arched brackets, finely crafted balustrades, and slate roofs. This refined and charming style was perfected with aesthetic details like the addition of flourishes and cornices, the use of posts to create hexagonal sections, and paint in a pleasing hue. The surrounding plantings—shrubs and perennials with fragrant flowers, strewn with a few topiary shrubs and potted flowers—also contribute to the atmosphere. This elegant decor, however, needs faithful maintenance since, unlike the rustic style, it does not allow for imperfections and must always be impeccable.

Above: Rising up from bushes clipped into balls and sheltering an Italian pot, the delicately worked structure of this little gazebo displays an indisputably romantic style.

The Pagoda

The Anglo-Chinese style of the eighteenth century has recently become "in," and the chinoiseries of old are inspiring more and more manufacturers to revamp, in their own way and with the help of present-day materials, gazebos to look like pagodas and tea ceremony pavilions. Evoking faraway countries and oriental cultures, these structures bring dreams of serenity and of a refined way of life. But this newfound taste for Asia is also perceptible in the popularity of the original flora of the continent: shrubs, perennials, and climbers acclimated to our regions are quite often used to create Asian-inspired decor. To make the most of these structures, it is best to choose exotic plants such as those used in England in the eighteenth century, when the Chinese garden was all the rage and this picturesque style, combining chinoiseries with curiosities, for a time swept away the English romantic garden. Today, examples of this garden style are rare, but the considerable choice of exotic plants offered by nurseries and an interest in Asian aesthetics and culture still motivate a good number of gardeners to add an air of the Far East to their garden. This might well begin with the building of a pagoda, which will probably have to be custom made, as these elaborate constructions are hard to find ready-made. With a little imagination, though, you can customize an ordinary gazebo with an arched roof by painting it red and black. Along with these typical colors, accessories such as lanterns and chimes will complete the Asian look.

Above: This small pavilion brings together the refined characteristics of the Asian style: black and red lacquer, a geometric frieze, and a pagoda-like roof. **Facing page:** Set off by a little steeple and an ornate upswept roof profile, this brightly colored, contemporary Chinese-inspired shelter sings against the emerald green of bamboo, with dwarf species used as a ground cover, sculpted in a series of waves.

Materials and Techniques

So now you're ready! You've decided to build a garden shelter. You've chosen the style, you've picked out the site—all that is left is to decide on the type of material and how to build it. These notes will help guide your choice and your first steps in the construction of your garden shelter. You will not find blueprints here, because each structure is different, adapted to its own surroundings, to your own abilities, and financial means. Each shelter is thus unique. You need only imagine as best as you can and, above all, dream.

Building the Walls

1
Straw Bales

SIDE VIEW

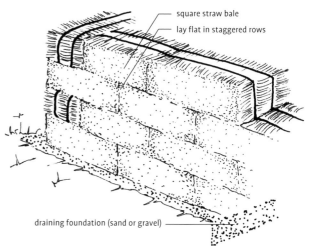

square straw bale
lay flat in staggered rows

draining foundation (sand or gravel)

Straw bales have long been an economical and ecologically sound material for building houses. Bales can be used to build walls in two ways: as infill, stacked within a wooden framework; and as a load-bearing wall, like bricks or cinder block. The wall can then be covered with a stucco-like coating to protect it from bad weather. For a small structure, the second choice is easiest: stack the bales in staggered rows on a flat and well-drained surface. Left bare—that is, without a stucco coating—these walls will last from three to five years. You will need to frame in the window and door openings with wood, and install windows and doors—perhaps salvaged from another building—in these openings. Top the walls with a heavy wood beam to serve as a roof plate, to which you can attach the roof frame.

HOW-TO

Use small square bales, bound together by bailing twine. Laying the bales on edge, so that the stems are oriented vertically, will limit the amount of water penetrating from the side into unprotected bales. Always set the first row on a bed of gravel or a row of cinder blocks to protect the bales from dampness seeping up from the ground. Stack the bales carefully, keeping them level by using a saw to eliminate uneven edges, so you create a perfectly vertical wall.

2
Stacked Logs

HOW-TO

Start by cutting the logs 12 to 15 inches long, and use a range of widths, since the small ones will fit nicely into the holes left between the thicker ones. Always build on flat ground that has been raked smooth, then covered with a layer of sand. Use large logs for the first row, then use all of the sizes together to create a solid wall. Strengthen the corners by crossing the logs, and be careful to keep the wall level and straight during every phase of construction. On the long sides, insert vertical support stakes, driven three to six feet into the ground, to reinforce the stability of the structure and to support the roof without putting undue stress on the walls. Every now and then, drive a nail from one log into the next to bind the rows together. Frame in door and window openings with wooden boards.

The felling or pruning of a tree produces a great quantity of wood that, cut into short pieces, can be used not only as firewood but also as an original and inexpensive construction material. Hard woods such as chestnut, oak, acacia, or ash are more resistant to moisture than soft woods such as willow and poplar. Don't use resinous wood such as pine, as the sticky sap will transfer to everyone and everything in the structure.

SIDE VIEW

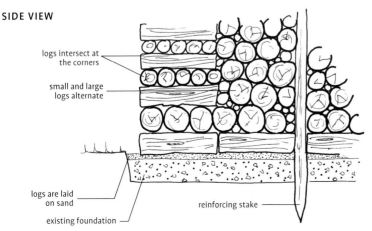

logs intersect at the corners

small and large logs alternate

logs are laid on sand

existing foundation

reinforcing stake

WINDOW DETAIL

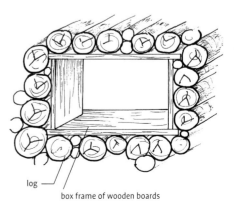

log

box frame of wooden boards

3
Cordwood

CROSS-SECTION

central space filled with insulating material

mortar joints

15-inch-long logs

concrete foundation

SIDE VIEW

smooth mortar joints

logs crossed at the corners

concrete foundation

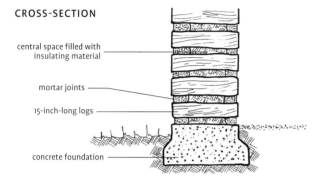

VIEW FROM ABOVE

log

central space (insulation)

band of mortar

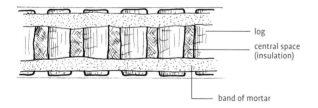

HOW-TO

Make a concrete foundation at least 15 inches thick, then lay down two strips of mortar on each side, leaving an empty central area between them. On this, lay a row of round logs, leaving a little space between them. Use a mallet to set the logs with a number of light taps. Then add two more rows of mortar and another layer of logs. As you are building, fill the central space with sawdust, wood shavings, or some other rot-proof insulating material, such as vermiculite. Smooth out the mortar as you go along to fill in the joints and make the wall waterproof. Continue until you have reached your desired wall height, and remember to alternate log directions at the corners. Use boards to frame out the window and door openings.

STACKING THE LOGS

whole logs

split logs

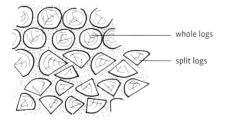

This ancient construction technique, which reappeared a few years ago in outbuildings and even residences, is based on building walls with whole or split logs set into mortar. The system is quite simple, environmentally friendly, and inexpensive, as long as you have a large amount of very dry wood, which is the secret to a long-lasting structure of this type.

4
Half-Rounds

When logs are milled to make boards, the first and last cuts, half-rounds with bark on one side, are usually thrown out as rubbish. But when salvaged, they can create a rustic siding attached, like boards, onto a wooden frame. Smaller half-rounds made of the branches of different trees, split in two and nailed onto wood panels, can create a very nice inlaid effect but are not long-lasting.

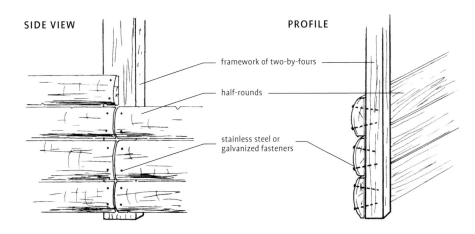

SIDE VIEW   PROFILE

framework of two-by-fours

half-rounds

stainless steel or
galvanized fasteners

5
Rough-Cut Vertical Siding

These boards, thinner than those used for wood framing, are generally made of pine that has been treated against insect damage and rot. Designed for framing out a roof or creating forms for concrete walls, to be discarded after the concrete has hardened, these boards are very resistant to moisture if they are protected from direct rain. Exposed to the vagaries of the weather, pine siding will turn a very pretty gray color, which deepens over the years. Even unprotected, it will last several decades without maintenance and will take on quite an elegant look as the grain, chiseled out over time, stands out in relief.

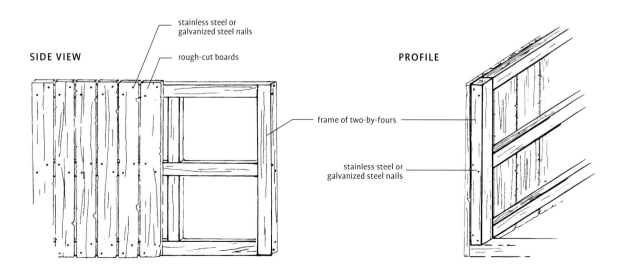

SIDE VIEW

stainless steel or galvanized steel nails

rough-cut boards

frame of two-by-fours

PROFILE

stainless steel or galvanized steel nails

6
Painted Vertical Siding

HOW-TO

Planks nailed to a wooden frame create the most basic structure for a garden shed. Made with studs set eighteen inches apart and additional space for window and door openings, this framework is fixed to a floor that has already been laid over concrete footers or cinder blocks. The vertical studs are attached to horizontal beams—also called girts—with galvanized nails or screws. Vertical siding does not offer much protection from slanting rain or wind, which can blow through the cracks between boards, but it is easier to cut and makes the structure look taller than it truly is. The walls can also be lined, inside, with a plastic sheet to block rain and wind.

As an alternative to treated pine, hardwood species qualified as exotic since they come from Indonesia (kempas, bangki-rai) or South America (ipe) are naturally weather resistant, but have a high ecological cost. Some better choices are resinous wood (spruce, larch, Douglas fir, or Scots pine) and broad-leaved trees (acacia, chestnut, oak, and ash), which can be found from more local sources. Their less dense wood does not last long unless it has been treated, however. Pressure-treated wood is soaked in insecticides and fungicides and then heated to a very high temperature. This procedure gives it a guaranteed life of ten to fifteen years, but if well preserved, it can last much longer, especially if it has been painted with a treatment that gives it additional protection against fungus and wood-boring larvae. Once painted, however, wood will have to be constantly repainted to keep up its appearance.

7
Board-and-Batten Siding

To reduce water seeping in and wind blowing through the cracks in vertical siding, you can cover up the small spaces between the boards with thinner strips of wood. Use galvanized nails or screws to fasten these smaller battens onto the framework that is exposed between the larger boards. More than just weatherproofing the structure, these battens have an attractive graphic quality.

SIDE VIEW

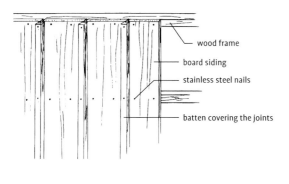

wood frame

board siding

stainless steel nails

batten covering the joints

VIEW FROM ABOVE

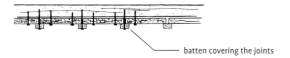

batten covering the joints

8
Plywood Panels

Some companies offer grooved wooden plywood panels that, once they have been fastened to a frame and painted, give the illusion of a wall made with individual boards, with much less work.

A WORD OF ADVICE

Easy and quick to put up, most plywood panels are intended for use indoors, where they will stay dry. However, there are water-resistant versions, such as the grooved T1-11 plywood or more technically advanced OSB (oriented strand board), better suited to damp areas and exterior use. It is still best to coat these panels with a water-resistant paint to lengthen their life, though they may still bulge after a few months' exposure to damp. To mitigate this inconvenience, do not install siding panels in contact with the ground, but leave a little gap below them, and do not paint them on the inside, so they can dry more quickly.

9
Rough-Cut Horizontal Siding

HOW-TO

The basic elements of these walls—that is, board siding and a frame—are identical to those used in rough-cut vertical siding, the only difference being that the boards are set horizontally on a frame of vertical studs. In some cases, the frame itself is enough to fasten the boards to, so extra vertical studs may not be necessary. This siding, with one board simply nailed in above the other, lets in more moisture and wind than would boards placed vertically. To reduce this, you can add interior waterproofing before attaching the siding. But it may be better to use one of a number of other methods, such as rabbeted joints, in which the boards fit together by means of a notched profile. The boards should always be attached to the frame with stainless steel or galvanized nails.

SIDE VIEW

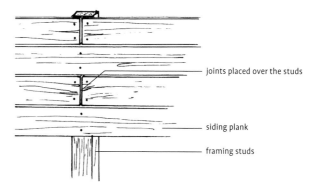

joints placed over the studs

siding plank

framing studs

METHODS

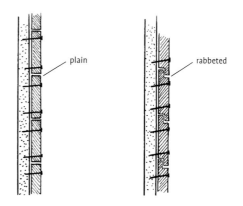

plain

rabbeted

10
Clapboard Siding

To better protect your structure from wind and rain, use overlapping siding. You can use the same materials as with regular siding, but overlap the boards slightly.

FRONT VIEW

framing studs

place joints over studs

siding boards

CROSS-SECTION

framing studs

stainless steel nails

overlap by a minimum of $1/10$ of a board

siding board

starting batten

11
Tongue-and-Groove Siding

In tongue-and-groove siding, boards are fit tightly together through the use of a profile where one side of the board has a channel cut into it, and the other has a piece that sticks out. This is known as paneling in interior decoration; the technique is the same for exterior work, the difference being that the boards are thicker and better able to stand up to exterior wear. However, there's nothing to prevent you from using pine paneling designed for interiors to side a garden shelter. Just be sure to treat the walls with a coating of waterproofing. They can easily be attached to a frame using nails—which will be visible—or metal clip fasteners, which will be invisible from the outside.

12
Natural Stone

Stone, left rough or dressed, is a practical material in the garden or near it. In the European countryside, a number of small buildings made either of cut rocks or large stones serve as shelters for shepherds, farmers, or vintners. The most famous are certainly the *bories* of Provence, round structures with pointed roofs rather like stone igloos. Real works of art—made of granite, limestone, slate, or sandstone, depending on the natural stone of the region—drystone walls require some experience to fit the large stones in place.

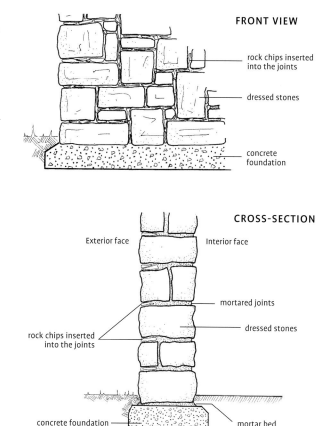

FRONT VIEW

rock chips inserted into the joints

dressed stones

concrete foundation

HOW-TO

There are a number of ways to build with stone, but all of them can be divided into two major approaches. In the first, the stones are dressed to achieve a flat, regular surface, so they can be stacked tightly, leaving the smallest possible joints, which are often left dry—that is, without mortar—at the front. In the second approach, undressed stones of different sizes are fitted together, with the fit adjusted with small fragments of stone. Here, the joints are larger, but always left without mortar, to appear as natural as possible.

CROSS-SECTION

Exterior face — Interior face

mortared joints

rock chips inserted into the joints

dressed stones

concrete foundation — mortar bed

13
Dressed Stone

14
Painted Stone

Structures made of large blocks, whether dressed stone or cinder block, are rarely considered garden sheds, since they are masonry structures, not the more traditional wood. However, when built on a small scale, these structures seem more like sheds, especially when they are refuges constructed out in the empty countryside. Legally, these are permanent buildings—as opposed to wooden shelters, which can be dismantled—and thus require a building permit. These are complex projects due to the difficulty of the materials—large stones, cinder blocks, bricks, and mortar—and require technical ability. Because of their weight, they must be set on very firm ground. Stone structures use the same techniques described in "Natural Stone" above, the only difference being that the blocks are more carefully laid to create even, regular walls.

The trend toward color in the garden, along with the need to cover unattractive masonry, has inspired the development of paints that can be used on brick or stone walls. Dressed stone has not escaped this wave of "renovation"—which can hardly be considered as such, since stone should never be painted. This material, more or less porous naturally, must be exposed to the air so that it can breathe and release humidity. To wrap it in an impermeable skin is contrary to the principles of stabilizing stone. Moreover, from an aesthetic perspective, it is absurd to hide the texture and colors of this natural material under a coating of paint. Porous paints do exist, however, and they may be applied if the surface is carefully prepared beforehand.

15
Brick

16
Stuccoed Cinder Block

Bricks, made by hand or industrially, solid or hollow, offer a great diversity of tones due to regional variations in the clay and different firing techniques. They are laid in a number of ways—with different equipment—the simplest being the running bond, in which bricks are stacked one on top of the other in staggered rows. For a more solid construction, metal ties can be run through the joints at regular intervals, or braces can be added. Another method is to lay some bricks, known as headers, perpendicular to the run of the wall. This technique ensures a perfectly stable wall, but one that is thicker and takes up more space. Building brick structures requires a little know-how, and the monitoring of the work by a mason is strongly advised.

Building a shelter in cinder block is another option that demands technical competence and requires the application of some protective coating or stucco to guard against the hazards of the weather. A stucco coating also covers any imperfections in the block that may arise during construction or quite simply hides the cinder blocks, since their appearance is not the most decorative. It can take on a number of colors, depending on the binder used. Use gray tones if the sand includes cement, and blond tones if you opt for sand and lime. You can also create your own colors by adding a pigment when mixing your stucco. To be able to successfully build a cinder block structure, you will need to install a foundation of reinforced concrete. For more substantial projects, create concrete pillars or fill hollow cinder blocks with mortar, which will assure the solidity of the building. For the openings, simply use the preframed windows and doors sold at home improvement stores, choosing those with an unusual look and small dimensions to keep the spirit of the garden shelter.

Raising a Shelter above the Ground

1
On Blocks

There are two ways to raise a shelter slightly off the ground, depending on how high you want. Using one cinder block, or two stacked, will raise your building 9 to 18 inches. To raise your building higher than this, use heavy wooden posts set directly on a concrete slab or plinth.

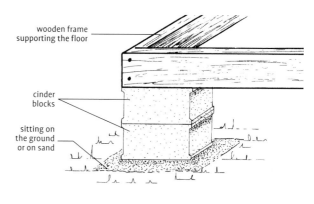

wooden frame supporting the floor

cinder blocks

sitting on the ground or on sand

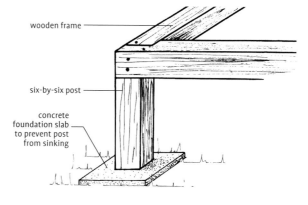

wooden frame

six-by-six post

concrete foundation slab to prevent post from sinking

HOW-TO

Even though the construction process for a raised garden shelter is identical to that for a structure on solid ground, the specifics of elevating a building on blocks or posts merit a little discussion. To perch a shelter on cinder blocks—the easiest route—set the cinder blocks on a bed of sand, placed every 3 to 5 feet, being careful that the tops of all are level. To raise the structure a little higher, make a load-bearing frame from pressure-treated vertical six-by-six posts, cut to the desired height, and attached at each corner. Place these posts on top of a foundation slab, or set them directly into concrete.

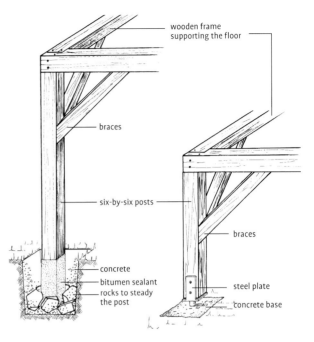

wooden frame
supporting the floor

braces

six-by-six posts

braces

concrete

bitumen sealant

rocks to steady
the post

steel plate

concrete base

2
On Piles

Lack of trees sturdy or large enough to support a structure is no reason to forgo a perched garden shelter. Built on piles and set near the woods, a shelter can give the impression of a little cabin buried in leaves. This solution also avoids putting stress on the limbs of a fragile or older tree. However, the choice, the quantity, and the placement of the piles should not be left to chance, and you might want to seek the advice of a professional before starting work.

HOW-TO

Although the basic principles for building this kind of shelter are identical to those for a structure built on firm ground, it demands special care. Be particularly attentive to the foundation that will hold up the structure. The ground needs to be stable and of the same consistency at all points, so that all anchorage points will match. For each of the six-by-six posts, set out at five-foot intervals, make a hole filled with cement to create a base in which to embed the metal plates that will hold the posts. You can also set the poles directly in concrete. Cut the tops of the poles off at the height you desire, making sure they're level, to support a frame of two-by-sixes or two-by-eights, on which you will set the floorboards. You can also leave the posts uncut, so they can serve as support for the walls of your shelter. Then add further support by inserting braces—two-by-fours set at a 45-degree angle between the posts and the frame—before you erect the walls and roof.

3
In a Tree

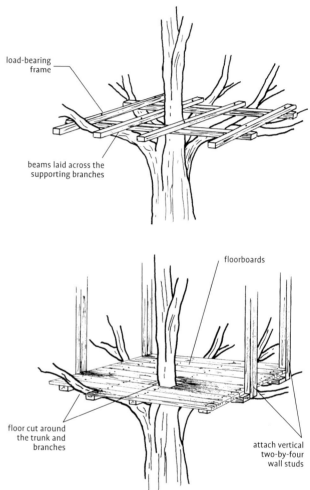

load-bearing frame

beams laid across the supporting branches

floorboards

floor cut around the trunk and branches

attach vertical two-by-four wall studs

A WORD OF ADVICE

If you use the branches of a tree for support, you must be careful not to damage the sapwood, or at least not weaken the tree with destructive anchors. There are a number of ways to proceed, such as bracing directly against the trunk and the principal branches with the aid of a steel collar; this allows you to fasten a frame to the tree and can be adjusted as the tree grows. Another system uses metal rods, inserted into the tree in a few well-chosen places where they will do the least damage, on which you can fasten your wooden frame. In a private garden, the simplest solution is to place the supporting beams on branches that are close together and somewhat horizontal, inserting a protective rubber piece between the beams and the bark. The platform thus created can then support a treehouse, but you will have to accept some shifting as the branches grow or sag.

Before starting to build a treehouse, make sure that the tree itself is solid and able to support such a structure. Some species—alder, willow, elm, and maple, for example—have brittle branches or a habit that does not lend itself to a treehouse. Take a look at the roots, the trunk, and above all the branches; how they attach to the trunk, their angle, their diameter, and their health all have an impact on the success of your structure. Think also about its position in the garden, particularly with regard to the prevailing winds. All these points are considered by professional treehouse builders, to whom you can entrust your project if you are not sure you can construct it on your own

Screening the Sides of an Open Garden Shelter

1
Trellises and Screens

HOW-TO

To use standardized four-by-six-foot trellis panels, you'll need to install horizontal laths between a gazebo's supporting pillars. The trellis panels can then be attached to these supports with thin wire. Another solution consists of stretching a cable, tightened by a turnbuckle, horizontally every three feet between the pillars, and attaching the trellis to this. In most cases, the dimensions of the standardized panels will not match those of your gazebo exactly. You can cut the trellis to the right dimensions or use scraps to fill in the extra space.

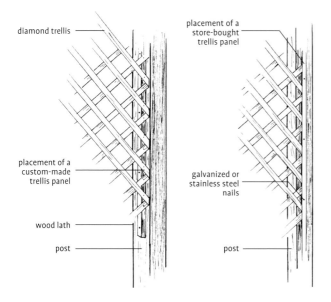

diamond trellis

placement of a store-bought trellis panel

placement of a custom-made trellis panel

galvanized or stainless steel nails

wood lath

post

post

Decorative screens and trellises are made with thin wooden laths, fastened together to create a panel of small square or diamond openings. They are designed to cover and close off the sides of a gazebo without blocking the view entirely, and to serve as support for climbing plants. Weather-resistant exotic woods can be left rough without any particular treatment, but pine must be protected by some paint or stain. Handmade custom trellises cost much more, of course, than the standard models that are available from home improvement and garden stores.

2
Bentwood

SIDE VIEW

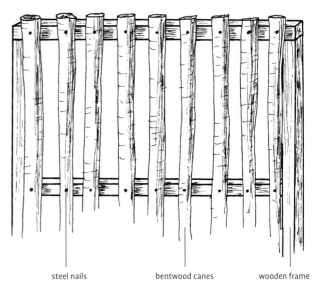

steel nails   bentwood canes   wooden frame

HOW-TO

Buy wood canes from a garden center, or make your own by collecting willow, hazel, birch, or mulberry branches. Wood that is freshly cut and thus still green is easy to bend into curved shapes, while older branches should be used for geometric trellises. For the latter, make a wood frame to fit the dimensions of your gazebo, but no larger than one yard across, to make it easier to handle and place it. If you opt for half-rounds, place the flat surface against the support and attach it with galvanized or stainless steel nails. Whole canes can be easily attached with metal wire. Arrange the canes horizontally, vertically, or on the diagonal according to your taste. Even in a sheltered place, wood is altered when it comes into contact with moisture, so be aware that the canes will have to be replaced every four to six years.

TOP VIEW

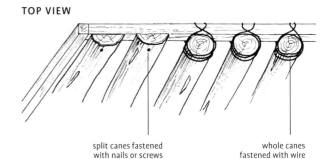

split canes fastened   whole canes
with nails or screws   fastened with wire

Pruning produces a great quantity of wood that can be to recycled to create rustic and natural-looking trellises. The branches most suitable to this use are those from more pliable trees, such as birch, willow, and mulberry. In Europe, chestnut is popular, as it is both supple and long-lasting. There wooden canes made from three- and four-year-old chestnut are sold with the bark still on, full-length or cut; they can be bent easily to make all sorts of frames but can also be used for decorative panels.

3
Lath

4
Forged Steel

Halfway between trellis and brush panels, lath produces light shade and gives a resolutely modern air to a gazebo, even though it is rooted in an ancient technique: wattle-and-daub wall construction. Easy to make yourself, this type of wall covering relies for its success on the choice of wood used for the laths, which must be very dry and sturdy, and thus not easily warped. A similar effect, as seen here, can be obtained with bamboo poles.

Sturdy and durable, forged steel requires special materials, especially welding equipment, to create trellised panels or even simply to fasten a piece to an existing support. A locksmith may help with making the metal strips, but forged steel's longevity justifies the services of a specialist.

HOW-TO

The laths you can buy at the lumberyard, now usually used for tiling roofs, are thin strips one or one and a half inches wide. They can be nailed to gazebo posts with galvanized or stainless steel nails, or fixed onto detachable wooden frames for ease in handling. A beige color when they are new, they rapidly fade to a silver gray. The laths never stay perfectly straight, since moisture tends to warp the wood.

A WORD OF ADVICE

If you opt for fine strips of steel for your shelter, treating them will cut down on the maintenance they need, which can be time-consuming. Galvanizing techniques considerably reduce damage from rust, which literally eats away at the metal. Even more effective, a coat of lacquer or epoxy paint offers very efficient protection on these structures. Although costlier to buy, pre-treated metal trellises need little maintenance.

Building a Solid Roof

1
Thatch

2
Wood Shavings

Thatch, one of the most ancient roofing materials, has resurfaced recently, after having almost completely disappeared from use. A thatched roof is commonly made of wheat straw—often replaced today with water reeds, whose saltiness discourages rodents—brushed and bundled into bunches, then fastened tightly to a frame. Resistant to frost, rain, and storms, a thatched roof should be entrusted to a specialist, as it demands a particular skill. On a garden shelter, this type of environmentally conscious roofing creates an undeniably decorative effect.

The bits of wood left over from planing and chopping wood make a cheap material to use as roofing. These wooden scraps make great insulation when laid on a roof frame. Sandwiched between poles and a sheet of plastic that makes the roof more weatherproof, over a few months they form a compact and dense mat that can block the wind. It is also possible to use shavings from a sawmill, if they are large enough. To make sure the wood scraps stay in place, do not use them on a steeply sloped roof, and cover them with bird netting so that they do not blow away.

3
Coppice

4
Half-Rounds

Some tree species such as birch or briars produce thin, pliable twigs that, when bundled together or woven into panels can make a roof that is rustic but impermeable. One must first fasten a plastic film or a bitumen membrane onto the roofing frame to make it perfectly waterproof. Gather a bunch of small branches of equal size—no more than a handful—bind them with wire, then nail them to a wooden frame, beginning at the bottom of the roof and working up. Lasting six to eight years, this natural covering, evoking primitive huts, brings out the rustic spirit of a garden shelter.

When logs are sawn into boards, slabs of various widths, shapes, and thicknesses are produced with bark on one side. Usually destined for the scrap heap, this cheap material can be used for siding, but also for roofs. These half-rounds, cut into fifteen- to twenty-inch lengths, can be fixed lengthwise to the roof frame much like shingles. In addition to being rather heavy—check to make sure that your frame can carry the weight—this type of covering has a rough look. It is also not very waterproof, so you will need to include a plastic film or bitumen membrane under it.

5
Shingles

Shingles of larch, chestnut, spruce, or red cedar can be used both to cover roofs and as siding. They should be nailed onto lath, which is fastened to the roofing frame.

HOW-TO

With an average width of eight inches to a foot, shingles are always placed parallel to the slope; that is, the grain should be vertical. Placed side by side, with each row overlapping the previous one, shingles on one row cover the joints between those on the row below. The nails used to fasten them are always hidden by the row above.

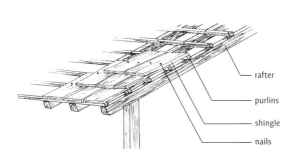

rafter
purlins
shingle
nails

6
Clapboard

The rough planks generally used as a support for tiles, slate, or tin, or as concrete form boards, can be diverted from these utilitarian functions to cover the roof of a garden shelter. Nailed onto the rafters in an overlapping fashion, much like shingles, they produce a graphic effect. But they are not made to be exposed to the elements for long, so you will need to replace them every three to five years, unless you treat them with a waterproof sealant.

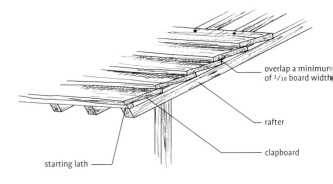

overlap a minimum of $1/10$ board width

rafter

clapboard

starting lath

7
Hand-Made Barrel Tiles

8
Machine-Made Tiles

Clay barrel tiles create undulating roofs reminiscent of Mediterranean regions. These traditional tiles, called channel or canal tiles, are shaped in a half-round curve; they are set on a support of triangular rafters fastened onto the main frame. One drawback of barrel tiles is that they are very heavy. For a wooden shelter, it is better to use round tiles with a lip on one side that hooks over a channel on the next. Since these overlap less, you use fewer tiles per square foot, which makes the whole roof lighter. Single-sloped shed roofs are easier to cover than A-frames. Not only are the latter more complex to build, but they also require a ridge cap at the top, which can leak.

There are numerous types of mass-produced tiles—flat, undulating to one side, or more or less curved—that can be used where classical clay barrel tiles are not consistent with the regional style. They are placed on purlins that are in turn nailed to the rafters of the roof frame. For small structures, such as a garden shed, they are quite easy to work with.

A WORD OF ADVICE

Salvaging tiles from a construction site is the cheapest way to roof a garden shed. Make sure that the tiles you get are ones that can be still purchased, or collect and store more than you initially need so as to have extras for future repairs. Newer tiles may have a different profile and will therefore fit poorly, inviting leaks. There are also metal panels that imitate the look of tiles, usually three feet across, that work well for roofs of structures such as a garden shed or covered playground.

9
Natural Stone

The flat stone tiles (schist, lava, or limestone) used to cover roofs in the south of France have a very decorative look, but their use requires considerable skill. This mode of roofing requires the building of a solid, load-bearing structure that can handle the additional weight of the stone. If you opt for a stone roof for your shed, engage a skilled professional roofer. Slate can also be used for roof shingles, which are thinner and simpler to install than stone. Typical in northern climates and often seen on historic residences and monuments, slate shingles are nailed through drilled holes onto purlins or battens. Easier to set in place than stone shingles, a slate roof needs no more skill than the spacing of the purlins and the setting of the shingles themselves.

10
Corrugated Tin

Long looked down on as roofing for agricultural buildings in the country, where they punctuate the landscape with rusty-hued silvery notes, these wavy galvanized panels have recently gained some stature. Now an "in" material, the tin roof is today appreciated and sought after for the subtle gray tones that come as the metal oxidizes, and the shades of rust that it acquires after decades of use.

A WORD OF ADVICE

Use galvanized nails to fasten new or salvaged panels directly onto a roofing frame or to vertical studs to cover a wall. They can be cut to any desired shape with a circular saw equipped with a blade for cutting metal.

11
Tar Paper

12
Asphalt Shingles

Quick and easy to install without any particular skill, corrugated tar paper panels come in a range of colors—green and terra-cotta, among others—that blend particularly well into the landscape and are quite suitable for garden sheds. The panels can be fastened onto the roofing frame, following the slant of the roof, with nails fitted with a thin plastic disk so they hold the material down without tearing it. Corrugated tar paper panels do not hold up to weight and therefore cannot be walked on. Peel-and-stick single-ply bitumen membranes, which come in rolls, are even simpler to install—they can be simply stuck onto a frame or plywood—and work quite well with shallow-pitched or even flat roofs. However, their black or gray color is rather plain, and leaves the roof looking unfinished. It is possible to find some versions in red or green.

These shingles are much more decorative than simple tar-paper membranes. Each shingle consists of a fiberglass mat reinforced by top and bottom layers of asphalt, topped with a layer of colored mineral granule. From a distance, this type of roofing is similar in look to slate shingles. Large-headed nails are used to fastened the shingles onto a sheathing of plywood that has been nailed to the roofing frame. Each row can also be bonded to the previous row to make it completely waterproof, especially on low-pitched roofs exposed to driving winds.

13
Synthetics

A world of high-tech roofing materials—polyester, polycar-bonate, and PVC—offer a smorgasbord of looks and uses. Opaque or translucent, these plastic panels are generally one layer, but some are offered in double- or even triple-ply versions. Polycarbonates are always translucent, and thus suited to covering conservatories and greenhouses. Corrugated versions range in profile from fine to very large waves—these last are not the best choice for garden shed roofs, because their profile is disproportionate to the size of the structure.

HOW-TO

Fasten corrugated panels to the purlins of a roofing frame perpendicular to the slant of the roof. A single panel—a standard size is four by eight feet—can usually cover one side of a roof, which saves you from over-lapping smaller panels and risking wind damage. The panels are held in place with plastic blocks inserted in the convex part and fastened with coach screws fitted above with an aluminum or plastic washer. This gives the panel support and, because of the compression, ensures that it is waterproof. Numerous accessories complete the installation of these plastic panels, such as a band of foam that follows the profile of the waves and makes the underside of these undulations airtight, or a ridge cap to cover the ridge of an A-frame roof.

14
The Flat Living Roof

HOW-TO

Make sure that your frame is strong and stable enough to carry the weight of a bed of two to four inches of soil and plants, which can add up to twenty or thirty pounds a square foot. If you opt for a flat roof, remem-ber that the horizontal look of the roof is somewhat of an illusion, since the structure holding the soil and the plants must be, at the very minimum, at a 2 to 3 percent grade to ensure that rain and snow melt can run off. This water can be collected by means of a gut-ter, and passed through a grill that filters out the dirt. Start by spreading a waterproof tarp 1 mm thick, such as a pond or pool liner, over the roof before lining the sides with boards that will hold the soil. Spread out a 3/4-inch-thick bed of gravel or expanded clay, which is very light, then cover this with rot-proof landscap-ing fabric. Then fill the bed with a mixture of equal parts compost and perlite or vermiculite (fragments of expanded rock) designed to lighten the load. Finally, add the plants (sedums, sempervivums, saxifrages, and grasses work well), spacing them at about sixteen plants per square yard.

Living roofs are the latest thing in Scandinavia, where virtual meadows spread over residential roofs. The practice, which once consisted of taking a sample of some turf from nature, has evolved today to bringing species from threatened biotopes into a new environment. Grasses and rock-garden plants like sempervivums are propagated in order to transplant them to living roofs, whose construction, insulation, and waterproofing have also considerably evolved.

This style of roofing, as it gains recognition for its decorative and ecological virtues, is spreading through Europe and to some extent America. Plantings on roofs decrease variations in temperature, absorb excess water, and help improve the air quality, especially in cities. Creating such roofs for larger urban buildings may be difficult, but it is quite easy to set up a living roof on a garden shed.

SIDE VIEW

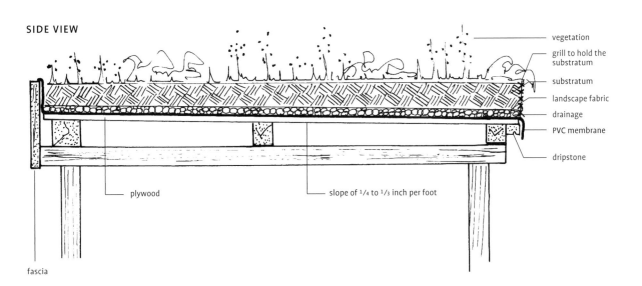

vegetation

grill to hold the substratum

substratum

landscape fabric

drainage

PVC membrane

dripstone

plywood

slope of 1/4 to 1/3 inch per foot

fascia

15
The Sloped Living Roof

A WORD OF ADVICE

When the roof is pitched, to stop the substratum from sliding off, make a framework of wood strips with a twenty-inch grid, drilling holes for PVC pipes through the wood to allow water to flow. On small roofs, you can fix laths horizontally across the slope of the roof for a similar effect. Use treated wood that can handle constant contact with moisture. The specifications for watertightness, drainage, placement of the substratum, and spacing of plants are all the same as for a flat roof.

A sloped living roof creates better drainage but requires more care in choosing plants, since they will be getting different amounts of sun depending on the slant of the roof. The pitch should never be more than 17 percent, or you will risk having your substratum slide away.

SIDE VIEW

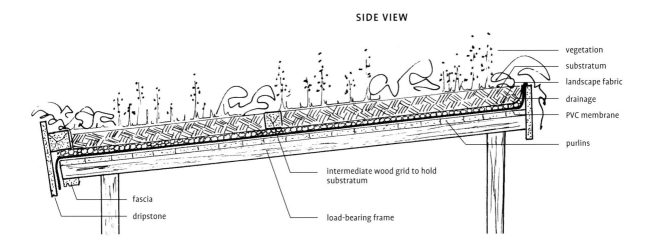

vegetation
substratum
landscape fabric
drainage
PVC membrane
purlins
intermediate wood grid to hold substratum
load-bearing frame
fascia
dripstone

Building an Open Roof

1
Lath

2
Wood Canes

An open lath roof set on a wooden roofing frame produces a contemporary ornamental effect. Treated pine laths, around an inch thick, are installed along the length of the slope and spaced according to the amount of shade you desire. Wood laths can be replaced with 1/2-to-3/4-inch-thick steel laths for metal-framed gazebos. Make sure that the structure is strong enough to support the weight of the metal; tubular laths can considerably reduce the weight. Don't forget that steel must be protected from rust with a paint intended for metal.

Whole or split in half, canes of wood such as willow or hazel can be fastened with galvanized nails to the rafters or beams making up the roofing frame, set perpendicular to the slope of the roof and at regular intervals. A progressive spacing, from larger at the bottom to smaller at the top, or the reverse, produces an original and very modern look. To anchor the canes even better and create a flatter surface, notch the rafters or beams where the canes will sit. You can also double fasten them with wire hidden by coir rope. After five or six years of exposure, canes that have been damaged by moisture or wood-boring insects will have to be replaced.

3
Bamboo

Resolutely contemporary, bamboo also brings an exotic note to the garden. This material can be used for the entire frame of a pergola or gazebo, from the ground up to the ridge, or only for the roof, which will then rest on a more traditional wooden frame. The advantage of bamboo is in its flexibility, which allows it to be used for rounded arches or for tunnels. Despite their suppleness and apparent ease of use, assembling bamboo canes can be difficult and demands considerable skill, which the Japanese have become masters at.

A WORD OF ADVICE

The longer the canes, the easier they are to bend to produce elegant arches. Harvest them while still green, since this is when they are at their most supple and easiest to bend. Do not nail them together—the fibers are brittle, and you risk cracking them—but fasten them instead with wire, hidden under hemp or coir rope. Practically rot-proof when left alone, bamboo canes stand up to bad weather and make an almost indestructible decoration.

4
Forged Steel

Just as with posts and walls, galvanized steel painted with epoxy allows us to create complex structures with elaborate shapes. Round tubular pieces look like massive wrought-iron work, but are considerably lighter and cheaper. With their double protection against rust, gazebos of galvanized, epoxy-covered steel are quite popular. But they are difficult works of art to create on one's own and may require the help of a welder.

5
Rebar

Unlike steel, which needs the skill of a welder, rebar in rods or welded into trellises is a very simple material for the layman to work with. Offered in six-foot lengths of different widths, these metal rods, which have a slightly twisted profile, bend easily to create vaults, tunnels, and arcades on their own or used with other materials such as wood or stone. Their rusty patina, which is part of their decorative look, is a given because it is impossible to paint them.

A WORD OF ADVICE

Rebar of a thicker diameter, and thus harder to bend, should be used to create the main frame of the structure, while thinner rods can be used to stabilize and decorate. A metal frame can be fastened to pillars or posts or rise directly from the ground, with the rods secured in a concrete base or driven deeply into the ground, before being tied together with the thinner rods with wire. Remember while working with rebar that the rods' ends can be sharp and dangerous.

6
Brush

As with a hut, a gazebo roof can be made with vegetation, salvaged on site from pruning a hedge or from cleaning up tall grass, bracken, or palm leaves. Bundled together, branches, grass, and bracken leaves are then attached to the wooden roofing frame of the structure. Palm leaves can be attached one by one to the structure. Although effective against the sun, this type of roof is vulnerable to wind and rain if there is no plastic sheeting between the frame and the vegetation, and may not last longer than a year.

7
Rough-Cut Planks

As with shed walls, using cladding to create a roof can be quite cheap. However, even when the wood is treated against wood-boring insects, long exposure to the elements considerably reduces its life span, which can be lengthened a little with a coating of waterproofing.

HOW-TO

Nail the planks to the rafters or purlins of the roof. When the boards are placed side by side, water will seep through the joints. Also, the boards can swell when wet, which can create unevenness in the surface of the roof. To limit this, it is better to overlap them. Always start at the eave end, or bottom of the roof, and use galvanized nails to fasten them. Remember that this kind of roof will only last five to six years.

8
Bitumen Membranes

If you are making an enclosed gazebo, you will need to have a waterproof roof. Though the technique for this is the same as for a shed roof, a gazebo's hexagonal or octagonal roof will make the job slightly more involved. Self-sticking bitumen membranes will make this job much easier for the layman, since they can be cut and adapted to all kinds of shapes.

HOW-TO

Bitumen membranes come in a number of colors in addition to their original black and can be coated with fine particles of natural or colored sand. Reinforced with fiber, these are sturdy and supple and can be cut to the shape and size that you wish. They can be stuck on easily, and joints can be covered with a strip of bitumen glued over the seam.

ACKNOWLEDGMENTS

The authors, Pierre Nessmann and Brigitte and Philippe Perdereau, would like to give warm thanks to the owners, gardeners, and landscape designers who opened the doors to their gardens and creations.

CREDITS

Front cover: Appeltern Gardens (Netherlands)
Back cover (from left to right): Coach House Garden (U.K.); Koelemeijer Tuinen (Netherlands); Landscape design by Serge Delsemme (Belgium); Jardin du Tomple (France)

Appletern Gardens (Netherlands): 71 (top)
Altlaurenscheuerhof private garden (Luxemburg): 7, 9 (right), 55 (bottom)
Arboretum de Balaine (France): 125 (left), 129 (left)
Architectures de jardin Bernard Joly (France): 122–23, 154 (right)
Bambouseraie de Prafrance (France): 40 (bottom), 41, 125 (right), 139, 154 (left)
Landscape design by James Basson (France): 60 (top), 75 (left), 147 (left)
Dominique Baxerres, gardener (France): 17
Landscape design by Philippe Burey (France): 8 (left), 9 (left), 40 (top), 45 (bottom), 51, 74 (right), 79 (top), 127, 144 (right)
Bridgemere Garden World (U.K.): 145 (left)
Pascal Callarec and Ronan Le Carvennec, Domaine de Courson (France): 15 (left), 27 (top)
Design by Blaise Cayol (France): 73
Design by Anthony Challis, Hampton Court Palace Flower Show 2006 (U.K.): 19 (right)
Landscape design by Joseph Chambel (France): 148 (left)
Philippe Chambon and Franck Nevel, architects (France): 14 (left), 33
Claverton Manor Garden (U.K.): 136 (left)
Coach House Garden (U.K.): 12 (right), 100 (left), 104
Courson Show (France): 132 (left), 134 (right)
Design by Claudia de Yong, Hampton Court Palace Flower Show 2006 (U.K.): 42–43, 134 (left)
Landscape design by Serge Delsemme (Belgium): 29
Design by Jean-Jacques Derboux, Jardin Gecko (France): 18, 56, 57 (top), 99 (bottom left), 124 (left), 135, 155 (left)
van Doorslaer private gardens (Belgium): 27 (bottom)
East Ruston Old Vicarage Garden (U.K.): 71 (bottom left), 85 (bottom)
Design by André Eve, Jardin de Pithiviers (France): 23
Exbury Gardens (U.K.): 11, 13 (right), 45 (top), 129 (right), 144 (left), 145 (right)
Festival International des Jardins de Chaumont-sur-Loire (France): 69, 71 (bottom right)
Gardens at Five Oaks Cottage in West Burton (U.K.): 24, 99 (bottom right)
Garden Le Beas (France): 46–47, 140
Hampton Court Palace Flower Show 2006 (U.K.): 151 (right), 152
Herbarium des Remparts (France): 26, 132 (right)
Design by Thomas Hoblyn, Hampton Court Palace Flower Show 2006 (U.K.): 28
Huntington Gardens (U.K.): 68 (right)
Jardin d'Anne-Marie (France): 119
Jardin de Bitche (France): 131, 150
Jardin d'Elsie (France): 13 (left), 87
Jardin d'Entêoulet (France): 31, 59, 74 (left), 89
Jardin de La Petite Rochelle (France): 68 (left)
Jardin Le Creux Baillot (Jersey, Channel Islands): 25 (top right), 92 (left), 99 (top left)
Jardin de La Poterie Hillen (France): 133 (right), 147 (right)
Jardin de la Noria (France): 110–11
Jardin des Paradis (France): 8 (right), 58, 153 (right)
Le Jardin de la Pellerine (France): 141
Jardin de la Pomme d'Ambre (France): 30
Jardin des Sambucs (France): 19 (left), 60 (bottom), 61 (bottom), 66–67
Jardin du Tomple (France): 75 (right), 81, 95, 128, 157
Jardin de Valérianes (France): 101 (right), 103, 108
Jardin du Viaduc in Burgundy (France): 106–7
Les Jardins Agapanthe (France): 83
Les Jardins de Castillon-Plantbessin (France): 121, 124 (right), 153 (left)
Les Jardins du Château Le Rivau (France): 142
Les Jardins de Kerdalo (France): 114
Jardins de Maizicourt (France): 112 (right), 113, 136 (left), 143 (right)
Jardins du Prieuré d'Orsan (France): 91
Kew Gardens (U.K.): 57 (bottom)
Garden of artist Peggy Kluck and gardener Licinio Flores (France): 130
Koelemeijer Tuinen (Netherlands): 54, 55 (top)
Le Mas des Câpriers (France): 77–78, 112 (left)
Design by Jean Mus (France): 86, 115 (bottom)
Design by Pierre Nessmann (France): 22
Park van Beervelde (Belgium): 99 (top right)
Passion Jardin show in Aix-en-Provence (France): 61 (top/landscape design by Italian Niccolò Grassi), 79 (bottom)
Landscape design by Anthony Paul (U.K.): 36–37
Pépinière Epimedum (Belgium): 143 (left)
Pépinière Labarthe (France): 98
Design by Hugues Peuvergne (France): 12 (left), 34, 48–49, 133 (left), 138, 148 (right); 38–39 and 126 (Festival International des Jardins de Chaumont-sur-Loire 2000)
Private properties: 25 (top left), 85 (top), 94, 117, 137 (right), 149, 151 (left), 156 (left)
Garden Roundhill Cottage in Chichester (U.K.): 14 (right), 35
Salines d'Arc-et-Senan (France): 21, 146 (right)
Landscape design by Michel Semini (France): 70
Sticky Wicket Garden (U.K.): 15 (right), 63–64, 90 (left), 92 (right), 93, 97, 155 (right), 156 (right)
Waterperry Gardens (U.K.): 109
Gaby Westermann private garden (Germany): 25 (bottom)
RHS Garden Wisley (U.K.): 146 (left)
Wollerton Old Hall Garden (U.K.): 101 (left), 105, 118
Woodhouse Garden (U.K.): 137 (left)
Yalding Organic Gardens (U.K.): 52–53, 90 (right)
York Gate Garden (U.K.): 65 (left), 100 (right), 120
Design by Christophe Yverneau (France): 115 (top)

Note: The following gardens were photographed for *City Gardens: Creative Ideas for Small Spaces* (Stewart, Tabori & Chang, 2008) and were designed by landscape artist Robert Bazelaire: 18, 21, 28, 54, 55 (top), 64 (bottom).